Even in the
Valley

Even in the Valley

*A Memoir of a Miracle -
A Journey from Cancer
to Hope and Healing.*

DEBBIE WILSON

Copyright © 2014 by Debbie Wilson

ISBN: 978-0-9855532-2-7

All rights reserved. Except as permitted under the U.S. Copyright Act of 1976, no part of this publication may be reproduced, distributed, or transmitted in any form or by any means, or stored in a database or retrieval system, without the prior written permission of the publisher.

Unless otherwise indicated, all scripture quotations are taken from the Living Bible copyright © 1971, used by permission of Tyndale house Publishers, Inc., Carol Stream, Illinois 60188. All rights reserved.

Scriptures marked KJV are taken from the King James version of the Holy Bible, which is in public domain.

Scriptures marked NLT are taken from the Holy Bible. New Living Translation copyright © 1996, 2004, 2007 by Tyndale House Foundation. Used by permission of Tyndale House Publishers Inc., Carol Stream, Illinois 60188. All rights reserved

Songs are reprinted with permission of the copyright holders:
"Even in the Valley" © *Thomas Peck Music (BMI)*
"Shout to the Lord" © 1993 Hillsong Publishing / Thankyou Music; © 1993, DarleneZschech/Hillsong Publishing, admin. Integrity›s Hosanna! Music

Front cover design by Lisa Hainline

Pictures of author by Margie Nielsen Photography

All other photos from the author's collection

DEDICATION

To my husband. You are my rock.

CONTENTS

Copyright iv
Dedication v
Preface............................ xiii
Chapter 1   The Premonition 1
Chapter 2   Signs of Trouble................. 19
Chapter 3   Premonitions Realized 27
Chapter 4   Happiness Invaded 41
Chapter 5   Replay from a Friend 55
Chapter 6   Sinking in Despair 65
Chapter 7   The Power of Prayer 79
Chapter 8   The Waiting 89
Chapter 9   The Journey for Answers 93
Chapter 10 Preparing for the Big Day 109
Chapter 11 The Day Arrives................. 115
Chapter 12 Unexpected News 121
Chapter 13 Stories of Faith................. 133
Chapter 14 A Nudge from God................ 139
Acknowledgments....................... 151
Verses Concerning Faith 153
Answers from the Author 161
About the Author 165

God will make a way where there is no way.
Through our Red Seas, God makes roads.
AUTHOR UNKNOWN

AUTHOR'S NOTE

Even in the Valley is the true account of a miracle from God. It relays the memories of the events before, during, and after my illness. Quotations and dialogue in the book are written for effect to capture the essence of what was said and are not necessarily the exact words of the speaker. To protect the privacy of others, some names have been changed.

PREFACE

When I was a little girl, I used to be fascinated by the life of the biblical prophet, Jonah. God gave Jonah a mission to go to Nineveh to tell the people there to turn from their sins, but Jonah didn't want to go. He feared for his life because he believed the very cruel people of Nineveh would kill him for bringing that kind of message, so he decided to run from God. He ran as far away from God's will as he could and ended up being thrown off of a ship and swallowed by a big fish.

As an adult, I had been running from God's will to share a message about faith and perseverance and healing. I was afraid of how it would be received, of the time and energy it would take to complete, of a lot of things. I had that same fear several years earlier when

I felt God's call to write my first book, *Sweet Scent of Justice*, a story about my sister's murder; it was the most difficult thing I had ever done. I didn't want to face a task that big again, so I ignored His call. I'm sure Jonah knew the call that God put in his life was a monumental task as well. That's another reason I think he ran from God.

It took Jonah three days of sitting in the belly of a great fish before he turned back to the Lord and decided he would obey Him. It took a lot of nudging by God to realize that I needed to stop running from His will and be obedient.

Chapter 1

THE PREMONITION

When I turned forty, I had premonitions about my sister's killer. She was only nineteen, a sophomore in college traveling alone late at night in her little blue mustang. Two serial killers confessed to the murder and the case was closed. But twenty-two years later, strong feelings consumed my soul that these men didn't do it. For some unexplainable reason, I knew in my heart that her real killer still remained free to kill again. I believe God placed that desire in my heart to search for the truth, and it turned out my suspicions were correct.

Six years later, I had a second premonition—just as intense, but this time it manifested as a strong intuition about my own near future—something unpleasant, even dreadful. I attempted to block out the thoughts, but they continually invaded my dreams during the night and mind during the day.

I believe both premonitions came from the Lord to prepare me to accomplish His will.

***

It was the summer of 2009, and it had been almost two years since the search for my sister's killer ended. She was just a sophomore in college when she was brutally raped and murdered. No more hunting for missing evidence, interviewing misleading investigators, waiting for DNA tests, or trying to enlist an elite force of international detectives to help solve the crime while working full time and being a mother of two beautiful teenagers. The efforts were fruitful. The killer now sits behind bars.

With the drama over and the adrenaline depleted, I seemed to have lots of down time to think about other things, so I began to take an interest in interior design and decided to remodel the home Todd and I built sixteen years earlier. Thumbing through a magazine, I came across before-and-after pictures of a remodeled home.

"Todd, look at this kitchen. The layout looks just

like ours," I said waving the magazine in front of him. "Look, they painted slightly different shades of the same color throughout their entire house. I think that's a really popular thing to do right now. Isn't it pretty?"

"Yeah, yeah, that looks good," he said, barely glancing at the pictures. Remodeling does not beat football for Todd.

"I think we should do something like that to our house. What do you think?"

"Yeah, that's a good idea."

"Todd, look at me. I'm serious. Let's remodel. Wallpaper is no longer in style and neither is this popcorn ceiling throughout the house."

He turned the TV down and looked at me with an "I give in" grin. "Well, if we are going to remodel I think we should build a pool."

"Did I hear someone say, *pool*?" asked Katelyn as she poked her head around the corner of the den. "What are y'all talking about?"

"Your mama wants to build a pool."

"That's not what I said, Todd."

"I do want to do some remodeling though. I want to scrape all of this wallpaper off and paint the walls a neutral color. I think we need to replace the counters in the kitchen, too. We can put granite on them. What do you think, Katelyn?"

"I think we should build a pool!" She shouted to Brittany who was in the back reading, "Brittany, come in here. Mama and Daddy are talking about building a pool."

"They are?"

"Well, not exactly, Brittany. I just told your daddy I thought it would be a good idea to remodel the house. He is the one who mentioned building a pool."

She smiled, "Well whoever mentioned it, I agree."

We had built our home ourselves sixteen years earlier when Brittany was just a toddler and Katelyn was a baby. Most of the work had been contracted out to a builder, but Todd and Daddy spent many months working with him to complete our first home.

When Todd and I were first married, we dreamed about one day building a house. We spent our Sunday afternoons driving around looking for the perfect lot where we'd lay the foundation for our future. We narrowed our search to one street only a mile from my parents' home. When a lot on the street became available, we bought it. A few years later, we began construction.

We spent many hours that June, walking the lot and marking the trees that had to be cleared so we could begin the building process. Like much of the land in the northern part of Louisiana, the huge oaks, tall pines, and budding dogwood trees crowded the lot.

A small hill near the center of the lot seemed to be placed in just the right spot for the foundation of our home. Behind the hill among all the small pines stood a majestic oak tree with its branches towering toward the sky.

Todd walked over to it, tearing off some orange colored ribbon.

"What are you doing?"

"I'm marking this tree. Why?"

"You can't mark that tree," I pleaded with him. "It's beautiful, and it's going to be the perfect tree to build a rope swing for the girls. It's right behind the house."

"See those branches? See how long they are?"

"That's why I love the tree!"

"Well, that's a good indicator that this tree's root system is also big. It might cause plumbing problems later, so I really think it needs to go. The last thing we need are tree roots growing around the pipes."

"But think about the shade it will provide for the house. It will probably cut our electric bill in half." I ran over and tried to hug the big tree. "Please!"

I knew I had won the battle when he chased me around the tree and kissed me. Then he took the orange tape and walked off to mark some of the small pine trees beside it.

Once the trees were cut, Todd used a tractor to smooth the ground. When the foundation was poured the walls began to take shape. I walked around the studs, into each room that would become the place where many photo albums would be filled and stored.

With my grandparents, Mama, Daddy, and the girls, Todd walked us through the layout.

"Brittany, this is going to be your room," Todd said as he held her in his arms and walked into the area. She wiggled down from her daddy and began kicking the puddles of water formed from the rain, splashing it everywhere.

My grandmother yelled, "Todd, you better pick her up before she gets soaking wet!"

Brittany took off as fast as she could through the tight wooden studs to get away from her daddy as he went after her.

My daddy took Katelyn's baby carrier out of my arms and carried her into the area that would be her room.

"One day you are going to be able to play with your big sister in your very own room. You can put your pretend kitchen over there and your bed can go on this side of the room." Katelyn smiled up at him while he was talking to her as if she understood every single word he was saying.

Week after week, I would take the girls to the house site and visit with Todd and Daddy while they took breaks from working on the house. Mama, Daddy and Todd's parents would come down to the house at night to build a fire in the fireplace and plan out the next day's work that had to be done. Todd's dad built beautiful stained rails for the upstairs banister and surprised us with a dining table he had hand carved from oak and stained with a walnut finish. The house took shape very quickly, and around Thanksgiving we were able to begin moving into our home.

The girls were in high school now and the house no longer had the charm it did when it was first constructed. It definitely needed a more modern look.

We decided to go for a full remodel, which grew us closer as a family, deciding as a team on paint colors and flooring and countertops. We labored together, scraping off wallpaper, and I supervised Todd over several weeks of tediously scraping off the popcorn ceilings.

One evening, we all went outside and used string and nails to mark off the exact spot where the pool would be placed and talked about all the good times we would have when the construction was complete.

"How wide will the pool be, Daddy?"

"Well, Katelyn, it's going to start about here," he would say as he walked off the distance, "and end here."

"We can have birthday parties, and Fourth of July parties."

"Sure, Katie, you can invite your friends over to swim any time. You won't have to wait for a special occasion." She ran over to her daddy and hugged him tightly.

"Your birthday's in December, Katelyn," Brittany kindly reminded her. "I don't think you will be doing much swimming at that time of year."

"We can put a table and chairs here and some lounge chairs here," Katelyn said as she gave Brittany a frown and went right back to walking the circumference of the pool.

Brittany looked over at me as I stood by a tree staring into the dusk-lit sky. "What's wrong with you, Mama? Why aren't you excited? Just think about it. We're going to have a pool—a pool! And we can swim in it any time we want."

"I am excited, Brittany."

"It doesn't look like it."

"I just have a lot on my mind."

I guess I couldn't hide from my oldest daughter my internal feelings, good or bad. She was right. I wasn't excited even though I should have been. After all, we were about to embark on something we had dreamed about doing for years, but how could I tell my family that I was scared and anxious about a feeling—a sensation in my soul that didn't make any sense to me? It was as though I had been having a premonition all summer long, and it foretold doom.

WITH THE PAINT colors and counter tops for the kitchen picked out, the only decision left was the type of flooring we would put down in the house. We picked out tile for the kitchen and wood flooring for the den. Just before the new flooring was to be installed, Todd was called out of town for a construction job. That meant Brittany, Katelyn and her boyfriend, Taylor, and I had to move the furniture from room to room each night so the workers could place the new tile and wood flooring throughout the house.

Even though Todd's job called for him to be away from home several days during the month, I never had gotten used to him being away from us. Every time he left for a job, a little piece of me left with him. After all, we had dated for eight years and had been married for over twenty. Our families had been friends for years. We had even ridden to kindergarten together, so we were used to doing everything with each other. Being without my partner hurt my soul.

Brittany smiled as she helped Katelyn move a chair from the den to the carport: "I think Daddy planned this out perfectly so he wouldn't have to help with all of this moving."

"I think you're right," Katelyn grunted as she lifted a chair to take it inside. "Don't you think he did, Mama?" They both laughed and waited on my response.

"What, Katelyn?"

"Are you even listening, Mama?"

"I'm sorry. I guess my mind is somewhere else."

My mind was somewhere else. It was right back to the place of doom and despair that confronted me daily. I reasoned to myself, *"Maybe I'm sad because Todd is gone, or maybe it's because I have to handle all of this while he's away. That's it. I'm just stressed because I have so many decisions to make by myself, and I'm just tired."*

No matter how hard I tried, I couldn't convince myself that I could blame Todd. I didn't understand it, but I knew my moodiness had a different source. A dark cloud continuously hung over me even when

I reminded myself how blessed I was to have such a wonderful family and a wonderful home and even more importantly, how blessed I was to have the joy of knowing the love of a Savior who was always with me.

Even in all of that, I truly felt like the Lord was preparing me for something, perhaps like He prepared me for Daddy's cancer. I had relied on my daddy for so much all of my life. God seemed to have given him an extra dose of wisdom, which he abundantly used to help me make most of my decisions about personal issues as well as work-related problems. He never minded helping me proof my letters and presentations or anything I needed. He was always a phone call away and I called a lot. As he and Mama traveled more often after their retirement, I had to let go of his coat tails and rely on my own judgment. I stopped to remember all those times, *"Was that God's way of preparing me for what I would have to eventually face when I lost him to the disease?"* I wondered.

When Todd came home from his job, he was pleasantly surprised to see how much work had been completed in the house. The painters had finished their work, the new floors had been put down, the granite countertops were in place, and the tile backsplash in the kitchen was almost finished.

He walked around, inspecting the work while I followed him from room to room.

"I think we can go ahead and start on the pool since there won't be very many workers in and out of the house now." He turned around and glanced at me. "You sure are quiet. Are you all right? What's wrong?"

"Nothing is wrong. Why do you ask?"

"How many years have we known each other? I know you, and I know when something is wrong."

"Nothing's wrong. The girls will be glad to hear that you are going to be starting on the swimming pool! They have been waiting for that day for a long time. I'm just ready to get started."

"Are you sure that's all it is?"

I managed a smile, "I'm sure."

Since we were nearing the end of the remodeling process, we decided to start digging the hole for the pool and putting a fence up to enclose the area. I had always wanted a white picket fence around the house, and I was finally getting one, of sorts.

The only thing keeping us from beginning the pool construction was one large tree that had to be cut down before we could begin digging. It was the tree that I had begged Todd to keep when we first constructed the house. It was large when we first built the house, and now it was even more majestic. It stood right in the middle of the spot where the steps to the shallow end of the pool would be located.

(Brittany and Katelyn around the old oak tree)

I couldn't imagine cutting the giant, old oak down, the one I saved from destruction sixteen years earlier. I spent hours planting beautiful azaleas around it when we first moved in the house, and images of the girls playing under it filled my scrapbooks and my heart. I told myself that we would make new memories around the pool, but as soon as I said that, a dark cloud of destruction trapped the thought from thinking it could become reality.

From the French doors in the living room, the girls

watched the men cut off one limb at a time, anxiously waiting on the tree to fall.

"Come over here with us, Mama, and watch."

"I don't want to watch, Katelyn. You know how much I love that tree."

"You are going to love the pool even more than that tree," she insisted, smiling at Brittany.

"I know I'm going to love the pool, but it just makes me a little sad. I can still see you and Katelyn running around the tree when you were little."

"Pool memories will be much better than running memories!"

Brittany patted me on the arm and said, "You won't ever lose those memories, Mama."

"I know."

Limb by limb they took the tree down, and when it was gone, a backhoe dug an enormous hole in the ground. They used elevation instruments to cut the exact dimensions of the pool, beginning with the shallow end. Then we watched as the slope to the deep end of the pool was formed.

After dinner that evening, we went outside to look at the hole that had been carved out of the ground.

Brittany walked the circumference of the pool, eyes large and lips happily parsed up.

"Britt, don't get too close to the edge."

"Daddy, I'm eighteen years old. I'm not going to fall in that hole."

"I know you're eighteen, but you still need to back away."

We stayed outside for quite a while that night placing the panels of the fence we had purchased in position so Todd and my brother, Steve, could put it in place after the pool was finished.

When the digging stopped, a slow steady rain began that would continue through the night into the early morning hours. We watched the walls of hard dirt carved out by the backhoe and measured perfectly to the exact dimensions of the pool become soggy and dangerously close to collapsing.

"I guess we disturbed an Indian burial ground when we dug up that tree you loved so much," Todd said putting on his rubber boots.

"What are you going to do?"

"I have to try to get some of that water out so the sides won't cave in and ruin all of the work we've done. It's the only thing I can do."

"You can't get that water out by yourself!"

"I don't have any other choice."

He finished putting on his rain gear and reached for the doorknob.

"Wait for me. I'll go put on some boots." I ran to the back, put them on as fast as I could, and threw on a jacket.

Todd stood at the bottom of the deep end with mud and water reaching close to the top of his boots. For hours, he stayed in the bottom of the hole and filled bucket after bucket with sludge, then lifted it over the eight-foot wall to me so I could pour it out close to the trees at the edge of the woods. He was so frustrated, and as I watched him struggle to remove the water, I was frustrated too—but the root of my frustration went much deeper than the hole where he was standing.

As I helped lift buckets, I stared at the mud and became more and more upset with each one I dumped. Tears welled up in my eyes. At first it was just a few tears that I attributed to my feelings of helplessness in the flooding, but I knew in my heart that wasn't the source of my pain. I thought maybe I was angry because we had spent so much money on getting the hole dug just right, and now we were in danger of having to start all over again. Even though I had all of those feelings, the tears represented more than that—they came out of darkness in the deepest part of my soul that brought on an unbearable sadness. I became frustrated because I couldn't understand my thoughts. Tears turned into sobs much like the torrents of rain already rolling down my face.

I didn't want the girls or Todd to see me upset, so I quickly walked under the carport, took off my muddy boots, ran to my room, fell on the bed, and cried uncontrollably.

"What's wrong with me, Lord? Why do I feel so sad? Why do I feel this overwhelming sense of dread, this cloud of sorrow?"

I asked God to help me understand. The thoughts never made any sense nor did they decrease in intensity. With each day, they consumed me a little more, and it frightened me.

"Why do you even care if the pool is completed? Why are you thinking about the good times you're going to have once it's ready for use. You don't need to get excited about the pool parties and the good times ahead. There's no need to do that. You won't enjoy the pool anyway. You won't enjoy it because you won't be here."

Chapter 2

SIGNS OF TROUBLE

Thanks to Todd's diligent efforts to remove the water during the storm and some much needed days of sunshine, the hole finally dried enough to begin the process of plastering the dirt walls with concrete. While he and some of his friends from work focused on putting the liner in place so the pool could be filled with water, the girls and I concentrated on the last of the remodeling projects going on inside the house.

"Brittany, will you come help me put the dishes back in the cabinets? I think the paint is dry now."

"I think it's Katelyn's turn to help."

"I think it's my turn to eat," Katelyn said as she popped some leftovers in the microwave. "Do you want me to heat some of this up for you too, Mama?"

"No, I'll get something later." I wasn't really hungry.

Eating didn't seem to be a desire or a priority for me. With all my running around to the paint stores, carpet stores, and other places to pick out items for the house, I rarely sat down long enough to eat breakfast or lunch.

I didn't think anything of it until I put on my favorite pair of jeans, and they seemed loose. The mirror and scale confirmed it. I had lost at least six pounds. I thought it was an added bonus for all of my hard work. I certainly had not been trying to diet. As a matter of fact, we had been eating take-out food for the whole summer since we couldn't get into the kitchen because the drawers and cabinets were being painted. I should have gained a few pounds. I stepped off the scale and began getting dressed, realizing that the extra inch in my pant's waistline was the first sign that my premonitions had entered reality.

And even though my summer workload at the office wasn't as hectic as it was during the fall and the construction was almost complete, my days at work seemed to be so tiring. Not long after I got to the office each day, I felt drained and very fatigued, and by the end of the day I felt exhausted. There were times that I couldn't even make it through the day without putting my head down on my desk for several minutes just to rest. I vowed I would start going to bed earlier, but even when I did get plenty of sleep, my tiredness never went away.

During those summer months, I opened the refrigerator and stared inside looking for something to eat, but nothing seemed appealing. Nothing tasted good either. Occasionally I fixed a meal and only ate a few bites. Just a few years earlier, I begged my grandmother to eat, but she just couldn't find anything that tasted quite right. Colon cancer had invaded her body, and taken away her appetite.

"Please try a few bites of fish," I urged, placing her favorite meal in front of her.

"That smells so good, Debbie, but I can't eat it. It just doesn't taste good to me."

"I'll go get you something else if you think you can eat it."

"No, I can't think of anything that I want to eat."

And then there was Daddy who had started feeling tired all the time and eventually stayed in the bed for most of the day before his diagnosis of esophageal cancer.

"Daddy, do you think you'll be able to walk next door to Nolan's birthday party?"

"I'll try to get there," he assured me.

It took all of his energy to get ready and come sit in a chair for a few minutes to visit with his grandson, only to walk back across the yard to his house not long after so he could rest.

"You're having the same symptoms as they had, Debbie. Face it. You have cancer, too!"

I tried to capture that C word and throw it out of my head, but it never went very far and always came roaring back with its final word on the matter: *"You won't be here long either!"*

After the pool and other renovations were completed, we spent the cool autumn evenings sitting on the lounge chairs watching the leaves gently float into the pool.

"I think we need to cut down some more of these trees before next summer," Todd said. "I can tell right now the pool is going to be a giant magnet for every single leaf."

"I love the trees. Remember? That's why we bought this lot in the first place—because of the tall oaks and the beautiful dogwoods," I said. "I don't want to cut another tree down. I promise I'll scoop all the leaves out myself if I have to."

"You say that now, but I know you'll change your mind once the wind picks up and they start falling by the hundreds."

"I promise!"

We sat in the pool chairs for hours enjoying the beautiful view. We were all so proud. Everything turned out just as we had envisioned it. Yet the longer we sat, the more anxious I became. I wanted to enjoy the moment, but I couldn't. Deep down, I knew I wouldn't be swimming next summer or lying out with the girls for much longer. That meant I wouldn't be scooping the leaves out of the pool next fall, either, like I promised. I just knew with all my heart that I wouldn't be taking part in any family event. I would be gone. My life would be over. So I did the only thing I knew how to do—lie in bed at night and pray:

> *"God, why am I feeling this way? Please take these terrible thoughts from me. Speak to my heart. Tell me I'm being ridiculous, even crazy. Ease my mind of the worry and fear that has overtaken me. I have two beautiful daughters I want to continue to raise and a husband that I want to grow old with. I'm too young to die."*

After my prayers, I felt no peace or relief from my impending death. Spiritually, I felt like I lived in an abandoned prison where my prayers hit the ceiling and bounced right back down to me. I had never felt so distant from the Lord I loved and to whom I had been so close. Every time I needed Him at a critical time, He was there.

This was especially true after the emergency c-section I had when Brittany was born. The doctors called her a "floppy baby" because of her low muscle tone, and because she wouldn't eat. I returned every day to the neonatal intensive care unit to see her, but going home to an empty nursery so delicately decorated for its tiny occupant pierced my heart.

Every day during that difficult time, I read scripture and prayed for her healing. I prayed daily that God would be near to us and comfort us. In my heart, I knew the great physician would cure what the doctors could not. After many weeks, she began responding normally, and the doctors told us her problems had resolved on their own. I never felt more close to God, and I knew that being in constant communication with Him led to Brittany's increased muscle tone and her ability to keep her food down. Within weeks she had a full recovery that the doctors could not explain.

Twelve years after Brittany's miracle, I traveled another long road, searching for my sister's killer. Along the way, I again experienced the Lord's faithfulness. At every apparent setback, He brought hope. At every dead end, He opened doors. I continuously prayed for His guidance, and He led me to the end of the road where healing and closure awaited.

I emerged from that valley of desperation and climbed to top of the mountain of victory. There I stood, grateful for all He had done. As I descended the mountain, reengaging in life, my family and work, I became content in my relationship with God and my reliance on Him—no more crying out for breakthroughs, no more meditating on scripture, no more claiming His promises to me. By the time I had my first premonition, I had walked far away from the mountain; our intimate bond had become a long-distance relationship.

I had become like the Israelites God led out of slavery. They watched with their very own eyes how God parted the Red Sea for them and drowned their enemies. They saw His glory follow them and His presence cover them, and they were blessed. But they walked away from His covering and His blessings. Like them, I saw the miraculous interventions of God in my life—and I walked away.

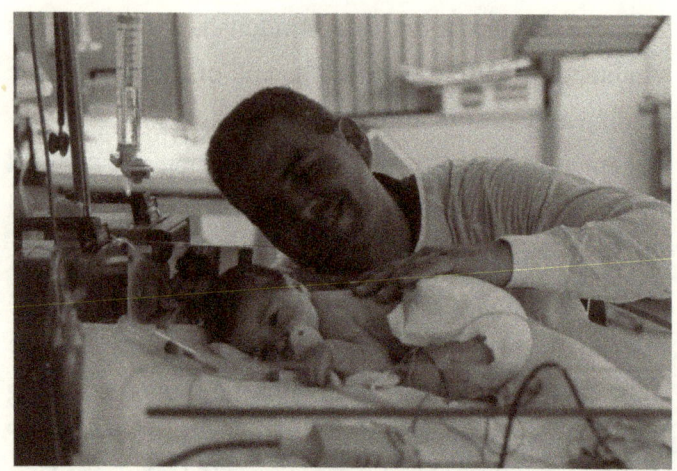

(Picture of Todd with Brittany in NICU)

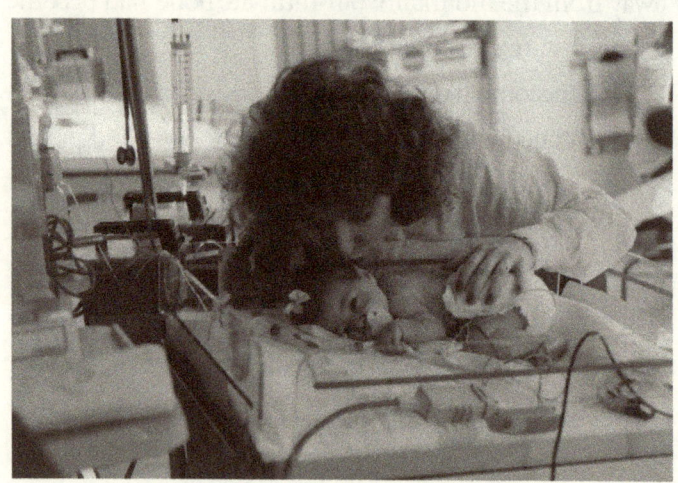

(Picture of me with Brittany in NICU)

Chapter 3

PREMONITIONS REALIZED

*I*N EARLY SEPTEMBER, my will could no longer hide the reality. It seemed like every thirty minutes I had to take a restroom break, and even afterward it felt like a faucet had been turned on high, but something blocked the water from flowing out.

I also got a bladder infection. I had battled them all of my life, so I self-diagnosed it and asked my doctor for a prescription for an antibiotic like I had done many times before. After a round of the medicine I felt better, but it didn't clear up the infection completely like it usually did.

Then, out of the blue, my right side began to hurt throughout the day—not a sharp stabbing pain, just a dull ache that I would sometimes feel while sitting at my desk. I considered going to the doctor, but as soon as I decided to make an appointment, the pain would leave and I put off the call.

The bladder pain and the pain in my side didn't get worse, but it never completely went away. It would come and go over the next few weeks leading into a new symptom—my left foot swelled. Every evening after work, I sat on the couch and propped it up. The small amount of swelling would eventually go away before I went to bed each night, so I still saw no need to see my doctor.

For weeks, I dealt with these issues without mentioning them to anyone. But very few secrets ever remain so. While sitting by the ice-cold pool one September evening, Brittany stood on the diving board pretending to jump off.

"I can't wait until next summer! I'm going to swim every day," she said.

"Brittany, you're going to fall in the pool and die of hypothermia. You won't be able to swim at all in the summer," Todd yelled out.

"Daddy, I'm not going to fall in the pool," she said smiling.

Katelyn just laughed at her sister as she sat down on a lounge chair. I sat down beside her and leaned back to relax. Todd quickly walked over.

"Debbie, look at your foot," he said quite concerned. "Take your sock off so I can see it."

I unveiled the secret to all, including myself. The swelling had grown to twice my foot size.

"You have got to go to the doctor. That's not normal."

I could tell by Todd's tone that he was more than worried, and deep down I knew that my body was trying to tell me something I still didn't want to hear. With both fingers in my internal ears, screaming at the top of my fears and emotions, I yelled, *"This cannot be happening!"* With great reluctance, and trepidation, I agreed to see Dr. Cox.

Most people who had my symptoms would have probably been to the doctor already, but I dreaded going because most of my experiences there resulted in bad news. After all, my mother, father, grandmother, and even my younger sister, Amy, had all been to see Dr. Cox, and all received the diagnosis "It's cancer." Even when I had a bad sinus infection, I waited as long as I could to go. I had prayed for God to give me a peace about going now, but I didn't feel any. All I felt was fear and worry. Todd would not let me delay the call any longer.

The morning I got dressed to see the doctor, I knew in my heart that I would not get good news. I prayed and asked God to let there be some other simple explanation for the symptoms—something that would be easy to fix—something other than cancer.

A cool breeze blew that September morning, so I grabbed a jacket before we went out the door. I didn't talk to Todd very much on the way to see Dr. Cox because my mind flooded with scenes of my funeral, my broken promises to clean the pool leaves, and my children living without a mother. These same thoughts were lurking through the crevices of my mind for many weeks, and now they found an open field to come together and bombard me during the short drive into town. In the waiting room, I tried looking through magazines, but it didn't help.

I realized that I needed to get back under God's covering. Being a Christian since early childhood, I knew what I had to do. I had to ask for His forgiveness for my wandering away, and sincerely ask Him to help me reestablish the close relationship I once had with Him: That's what the Israelites did, and that's what I did. So, finally, in the waiting room, I silently prayed,

"God, please let me feel your closeness again. I know you have never left me. I am the one who has moved

away from you. I need you now more than ever, dear Lord. Please let there be some simple explanation for my symptoms. God, please don't let there be anything seriously wrong with me."

I pleaded over and over until the nurse brought us to meet Dr. Cox.

"What can I do for you today, Mrs. Wilson?"

"Hello, Dr. Cox."

After I went through my symptoms and answered all of his questions, he handed me a prescription and said, "I want you to go over to the hospital and have a CAT scan done because I believe the problems you're experiencing are related to your kidneys. The nurse will call and get a time scheduled for you. After you have the scan done, I want you to bring the film back here and I'll take a look at it. Then we'll talk."

"Do you think we can get it done today?"

"We will get the first available time," he said, smiling before leaving the room. I turned to Todd with a solemn gaze of grief. He knew how much I hated every minute of all the CAT scans Brittany had.

As I got dressed, the nurse told me we could go straight to the hospital and do the scan. I bowed my head and let out a sigh—*"I don't like it, but finally I'll get some answers."*

I have always been a big baby about hospitals,

needles, and anything else related to doctor visits, but I was ready to get it over with. I now wanted to know.

"I have a bad feeling about this," I told Todd on the way to the hospital. "I just know it's going to be bad news."

"Why are you even talking like that, Debbie? You don't know what's wrong. Let's just wait and see what they find, and then we will deal with whatever comes our way. We can handle whatever we find out."

"I know we can deal with it, but I just want you to know I don't think it's going to be good."

"Let's don't borrow trouble."

Todd had always been my rock that I could depend on, even since our first date in Junior High. I needed his strength for the battle we were about to face.

When we entered the hospital we walked up to the front desk and completed all the paperwork for admissions.

"You need to go to x-ray on the first floor. Just take the elevator over there," the nurse said, pointing to the corner of the room. When the elevator doors closed, I smiled at Todd even though I felt in my heart I was about to begin a dead-end journey.

It turned out that the CAT scan itself was not as difficult as the drive back to Dr. Cox's office. The cause of my premonition lie embedded on the CD in my hand. A few miles seemed to take hours. The drive felt like the time my sister, Amy, and I got in an inflatable boat and rowed around in the ocean. While we headed back to shore and almost arrived, for a split second we caught a glimpse of a six-foot wave. It rose up under our boat and dumped both of us out and pinned us on the ocean floor. Life sometimes knocks us out and pins us down just like that big wave. We feel like we can't come up for air. That's how I felt in the car at that very moment—I couldn't breathe.

I knew I wouldn't enjoy the pool or the good times with the girls. I knew I wouldn't grow old with my husband. All of my premonitions were coming true. I had faith in the promise of going to heaven when I died of cancer, but I still didn't want to suffer—I just wanted to stay with my family here on earth for awhile longer.

"Debbie, you and Todd can go on back to his office," the receptionist said only a few minutes after arriving back at Dr. Cox's office. "He'll be with you in just a minute. He's finishing up with another patient."

We stepped into the room and maneuvered around the few pieces of furniture without bumping into something to get to the plastic orange chairs along the wall. The large wooden desk held medical books stacked so high that they seemed to take up three-fourths of the space in the room. A bookcase in the corner housed even more books as well as some framed certificates. As my eyes moved from one side of the room to the other, I noticed family portraits on the wall and a framed Scripture verse hanging right below them. I walked over to read the verse.

> But they that wait upon the Lord shall renew their strength; they shall mount up with wings as eagles; they shall run, and not be weary; and they shall walk, and not faint (Isaiah 40:31 KJV).

As I imagined stepping out of the office and onto eagles' wings, the door swung open. Dr. Cox walked into the room and sat down behind his desk. I squeezed Todd's hand as we both fixed our eyes on him trying to determine whether his wide eyes meant good news or bad news.

"Mrs. Wilson, I looked at your CAT scan, and I know it's not the news you wanted to hear." Without hesitating, he laid it out straight, "The scan shows a large mass in your right kidney. There's also a mass in the adrenal gland above your kidney."

I had already been warned all summer. It should

not have been such a shock, but I felt all my breath leave, as though I'd been kicked in the chest.

I looked up at him, "Is it cancer?"

"Come with me and let me show you the scan."

He walked down the hallway to another area where he turned to a computer screen and pointed to an image of my kidneys with the tip of his pen.

He repeated, "There is a large mass in your right kidney and also in the adrenal gland just above the kidney. The mass has almost completely taken over the entire kidney as you can see here." He pointed to the screen and showed us the outline of the tumors.

I asked again, "Is it cancer, Dr. Cox?"

He looked at me as if he didn't want to say it, but he replied, "The symptoms you are experiencing—the night sweats, lower back pain, fatigue, and weight loss along with the clear image of the tumors all indicate that it is cancer."

I wanted to melt into the floor and disappear from the whole situation. I didn't want to go through all the tests Daddy had to endure or the endless waiting on their results only to be officially diagnosed with cancer. I especially didn't want to go through the pain and suffering I saw Daddy and my grandmother endure before they went to be with the Lord.

Dr. Cox immediately asked about my preference

for a surgeon and named off doctors in the area, but his words were not making any sense to me.

Todd interrupted him and said, "Dr. Cox, can you get us in at M.D. Anderson?"

Both of us were all too familiar with the wonderful cancer facility in Houston, because Daddy had spent the last month of his life there when the doctors determined his cancer was in its final stage.

"I can certainly give them a call and see what I can do to get her an appointment. My nurse will get in touch with the hospital, and she'll call you when she has some news."

I was listening, but not really hearing. I was thinking about the day Daddy's doctor gave us his diagnosis at M.D. Anderson: "Mr. Whorton, your cancer is in the last stage. There really isn't a lot we can do for you except keep you comfortable." But he did leave Daddy with some hope: "When we first met, you told me about your strong faith in God. It will be your faith that will sustain you through this time."

Daddy didn't shed a tear, but Mother and I began sobbing. Daddy just smiled as he looked at the doctor and said, "Thank you for your time." My daddy was such a strong Christian and his faith never wavered even in the last days of his life. He never got angry with God, and he kept a smile on his face until the very end.

I left the room where Mother and Daddy were still trying to comprehend the devastating words, and began the long walk through the maze of hallways to the sky bridge that connected the hospital to the hotel. It was December. Decorated trees appeared here and there, and beautifully lit garlands draped the doorways. They reflected joy—a celebration of the gracious gift to us of God's son. Yet, as I walked along the bridge, I passed doctors in their green scrubs and patients in wheel chairs, and I wondered as I passed them, *"Can you see through to my soul to know that my life has just been crushed to the very core?"*

When I finally arrived at the hotel, I walked as fast as I could to the other side, rounded the corner, and pushed the button to the elevator, hoping it would be empty so I could release the pain in private. The doors opened to several people awaiting my entry. *"If my daddy could keep his composure, so could I."*

I stepped off the elevator onto my floor and ran to the room. I wanted the smallest, darkest place I could find to be alone and cry out to God in my brokenness. I ran into the bathroom, shut the door, and fell to my knees; there the tears poured. As I lay on the cold floor, I cried out loud to God to comfort me.

When I had no more tears, I begged the Lord to bring a scripture verse to my mind that would ease my pain. I knew many verses from the Bible because I had grown up in church hearing them read weekly. Since I was a little girl, I had meditated on and studied them during regular Bible studies. But now, my mind was so numb I couldn't think of one single verse.

"God, please! Lord, please give me a verse to comfort me and ease my pain," I begged.

In the quiet stillness of the dark, a verse from Psalm 23 came into my mind. I softly yet brokenly recited it aloud, "Yea, though I walk through the valley of the shadow of death, I will fear no evil; for you are with me; your rod and your staff they comfort me."[1]

The tears poured again. I knew what God was telling me. I would have to endure the death of my father, but the Lord, my heavenly father, would be with me. He would carry me and comfort me through it all.

Dr. Cox led us back to his office to talk to his nurse about our trip to Houston. As I sat there with Todd holding my hand and tears flowing down my cheeks, I looked again at the framed verse from Isaiah 40:31: "But they that wait upon the Lord shall renew their strength;

they shall mount up with wings as eagles; they shall run, and not be weary; and they shall walk, and not faint."

I knew exactly what it meant now. My faith in the Lord as my comforter would see me through this trial, just as He had seen me through the pain of my dad's final days, the murder of my sister, the search for her killer, the ailment of my first child, and all the other valleys in my life.

As the nurse started instructing us, I wanted to cry like I had done in that dark, cold bathroom, but I composed myself. She told us she'd be in contact as soon as the appointments were made, so Todd and I left, realizing we were about to begin a new journey of faith and trial, together as one.

(Picture of Daddy with Brittany and Katelyn after the new house was built)
(Left to right: Brittany, Katelyn, and Daddy)

Chapter 4

HAPPINESS INVADED

"Todd, please take me to the church."

"Are you sure you want to go now?"

"Yes, I'm sure. Please take me to see Brother Cal."

Brother Cal had been our pastor for several years, and I wanted to let him know that I desperately needed his prayers. I wanted everybody in the church to know what I was going through, so they could all pray for my healing and comfort.

I believed in the power of prayer because I saw how God had answered prayer in the past, even though His answers weren't always what I wanted. I prayed so hard that God would heal Daddy from his cancer, but God chose not to heal him the way I wanted him healed. Instead Daddy was healed when he entered heaven and no longer had to suffer from the pain that his cancer had tormented him with on this earth.

When we arrived at the church, the secretary greeted us with her usual smile that quickly turned to a serious gaze.

"Is Brother Cal here?" I asked through my tears.

"Sure, Debbie, y'all can go on back to his office."

Brother Cal must have heard us when we walked in because he was already making his way around his desk to greet us. I practically fell into his arms crying.

"What's wrong?"

Todd spoke up, "We just got some very bad news. The doctor has diagnosed Debbie with kidney cancer."

I looked at my pastor and said, "I want you to know that I'm okay. I'm fine with this. I know where I'm going if I die. Even though I don't want to die, if I do die, I know I will be alright. I know I will go to heaven. It's just the girls. I don't know how we are going to tell the girls."

Tears rolled down his cheeks just as they were rolling down ours.

"I want to pray with you."

Todd fell to his knees in prayer while Brother Cal reached his arm around my shoulder and asked God to give us the comfort that we needed. He prayed for God's healing hand to heal me, and he asked the Lord to be with us as we told the girls the terrible news.

After he prayed for us he said, "Debbie, you know I'm here for you if you need anything. You can call me at any time, and I'll come and pray with you. If it's in the middle of the night, you just call, and I will pray with you over the phone. If you want me to go to the house with you and Todd to be with you when you tell the girls, I will."

"Thank you, Brother Cal, but I think it's better if we tell them ourselves. We appreciate the offer though."

"I am serious now. Call me if you need me in any way."

As we headed home, our hearts were so heavy that we couldn't speak to each other. We had several hours before the girls got home from school, so I had a lot of time to reminisce.

I began to think about my grandmother and her trial with cancer. Since my mother worked, my grandmother practically raised me, so I was heartbroken when I heard that her cancer returned without any hope from the doctor for healing.

When I got home after dropping her off at her house from that last doctor's visit, I told Todd through many tears how much I would miss her.

"Debbie, she's here right now. Love her while she's here. She's not going to die today."

I knew he was right, so I spent as much time as I could with her. She and my grandfather relied on their faith in God to give them the strength they needed to cope with her illness, and so did I.

During those difficult days I read my Bible every day because I wanted to be as close to God as I could possibly be. I knew through His words He could send me comfort for what I would experience in the months to come with my grandmother.

Cancer would not be taking my life that day either, and I was determined to get as close to my Savior as I could. I also knew I wanted to make every moment of every day I had left with my family count.

(Picture of my grandmother and grandfather)

On the ride home from Dr. Cox's office, I thought about the practical side of dying, what it would mean to my family.

"How will Todd and the girls make it financially? Will my life insurance be enough money so they won't have to worry about finances?"

As soon as I walked in the door, I went straight to the kitchen and began looking through all the file folders in the desk drawer. Todd's hand covered my shoulder with his warmth as he walked up behind me.

"What are you looking for?"

"I'm looking for my life insurance policy. I know I have it in a file folder here somewhere." I pulled several folders from the drawer and searched through them.

He took the folders from my hands. "Don't talk like that, Debbie. Don't even think like that. You don't know what's going to happen. Look at your mom. She has survived two rounds of breast cancer, and Amy has fought breast cancer and won, too."

I looked at him quite seriously and said, "We are going to have everything lined out just in case I lose this battle, because it's too important that you're able to take care of the girls if I'm not here."

He grabbed me. We hugged. The tears flowed, again.

I put the folder on the counter, and we stood in the kitchen and prayed together. We prayed that God would be with the girls and us as we faced the fight together.

It was homecoming week at the girls' high school, and Brittany and Katelyn were so excited about the ongoing activities. I didn't want to invade their happiness with the news that their mama had a life-threatening disease. I wished I could just keep it a secret for just the week, so I wouldn't ruin their excitement, but I knew I couldn't. In our small town, news gets around quickly, and I didn't want them to somehow hear it from someone else.

While waiting for them to get home, all of the life events I would miss with my children overwhelmed me with sorrow. In desperation, I bargained with God: *"Lord, if you'll leave me here on this earth, I'll do so much for you. I will do more than I've ever done before. I have so much to offer you. I'll teach others about your goodness. I'll sing songs about your mercy and your grace."*

In reality, I knew He didn't need me to do any of His work. It was the other way around. I needed Him. I had always needed Him, through the good times in my life and the bad times.

I continued talking to Him, *"God, please help me*

tell the girls without getting too upset, and please comfort them when they hear the news." In between these requests, I also asked over and over, *"Deliver me from cancer if it is your will. I know you might choose to deliver me from it like you delivered my father—through death into life everlasting with you. If that is your will, then I accept it, but if there's any way to remove this destruction in my body and heal me, please do."*

I knew that the point of my deepest hurt might be the point at which He could use me the most to draw others to Him, but another side of me didn't want to hurt. I wanted to be free of the dreaded disease and free from the worry of death, and quickly.

I thought about the story of David and Goliath in the Bible. David asked God to be with him to help him conquer a giant named Goliath. David picked up a rock and his slingshot and conquered Goliath with a single stone and God's help. My giant was cancer and my hope was in the rock that would bring my giant down—the Rock of Ages—the Great I Am.

Todd and I kept sitting in silence until the door opened. Katelyn came running by us with books in hand headed straight to her room. Brittany wasn't too far behind her.

"We're going to try on our dresses for homecoming. We want you to see them. Don't leave the den now. We'll be right back."

After a few minutes, they both came rushing back with their homecoming dresses on for us to see. Katelyn's long blue dress matched the color of her eyes perfectly.

"Do you like the color, Mama?"

"I love it. It really makes your beautiful eyes stand out."

Brittany twirled around in her plum, floor-length dress as she entered the room and said, "I think my dress looks like it's from Victorian days. Don't you think so?"

"It's gorgeous Brittany," I said, straining a smile.

I knew I had to hurry and tell them, or I would break down and cry. They were both talking nonstop about the excitement of the day when I interrupted them, "Please girls, sit down so I can talk to you."

Katelyn's whole demeanor changed. Her eyes widened and she asked, "What's wrong?"

I knew Katelyn could sense our sadness even before I said anything.

"Mama went to the doctor today," Todd said.

Brittany sat down slowly beside her daddy. "What did he say?"

"The doctor said Mama has kidney cancer."

They both fell into my arms and cried. I held them, fighting back the tears.

"Are you going to die, Mama?"

Brittany knew that in our family the word cancer was like a death sentence because we had lost my grandmother and my daddy within a two-year span.

"What's going to happen, Mama?" Katelyn said, with tears pouring.

"I don't know, but I do know that I am okay with whatever happens. I know where I'm going if I die, and I'm not scared." They both hugged me, my shoulders becoming wet with their tears.

"It's okay. It's okay," I said, trying to comfort them.

"Girls, we do know this. God is going to be with Mama. We are going to go to the best doctors to get the best treatment available."

I reassured them that God was in control, and we would lean on Him for support. I finally got them to talk some more about the excitement of homecoming week and the activities of the day, but we all knew the weeks ahead were not going to be easy.

"We will take one day at a time. God is in control, and we will depend on Him."

We all lifted up prayers that night, unified as a family, with heavy hearts.

Todd's Prayer

Lord, Debbie and I have loved each other for so many years that I can't even imagine my life without her. I haven't been able to leave her side all day. I can't seem to get close enough to her even when I hug her tightly. I don't know how much time we have left together, and what about the girls, Lord? You know the impact on their lives will be so great! I want Debbie to be there for them. They need her so much, Lord. You know how special she is to me, God. Please let her live. I fell to my knees today in Brother Cal's office, and Lord that's where I'll stay if you will hear our prayers and heal her.

Brittany's Prayer

Lord, when Mama told us tonight that she had cancer, I was so scared and full of sadness. Mama has always been a guide for me, and she has been there for me through all of my struggles. I don't know what I would do if I lost her. But now for some reason you have given me an assurance that everything is going to be okay if I just trust in you. I praise you Lord for giving me the peace that has put a song in my heart and a smile back on my face.

Katelyn's Prayer

Dear Heavenly Father, I don't want my mama to leave me. Did she get this disease because of something wrong that I did? I just want to know that when I wake up she is going to be here, Lord. The world was moving in slow motion when she gave me the news today. God, nothing that had mattered to me before is important any more. Even Taylor wouldn't be able to comfort me from the sadness I feel. Not having answers is the worst part. I just want to spend every day with her until we know more about her illness. All I can think about is what life would be like without her. Please heal her, Lord.

(Brittany in her dress next to the new pool)

Happiness Invaded

(Katelyn in her dress in our newly remodeled den)

Chapter 5

REPLAY FROM A FRIEND

"I HAVE AN IDEA," Todd said leaning over the couch to grab my hand.

The warmth of his hand in mine and the vibrating purrs of our cat, Happy, next to my chest, revived me from a deep sleep. With a half-sarcastic yawn, I asked, "Does your idea have anything to do with rewinding time so that I won't be in this situation?"

"Baby, I would do anything to take this from you, you know that, but that's not my idea."

"What is it then?"

"Why don't we call Jim? Maybe he can take a look at the film and see something the other radiologist and Dr. Cox didn't see."

He hurried out of the room to get his phone. I just sat there in silence trying to stop the video in my head from replaying the events of the day. I wanted to smash the signal so I wouldn't have to think.

Todd yelled from the bedroom, "He wants us to meet him at his house. Do you think you can be ready to go over there in fifteen minutes?"

"That's fine. Tell him we'll be there in a few minutes."

I could physically get myself ready, but I didn't know if I could mentally prepare myself for hearing the news again. I went into the bedroom and put on some fresh makeup to hide my red face and puffy eyes. It probably didn't work.

Jim was one of the leading radiologists in the area. He had an excellent reputation for getting things right when it came to reading scans. He was also a very good family friend. Our daughters had taken dance with his daughter since they were little, and during football season we were usually together watching LSU play somewhere along with other friends. Todd and I both trusted his judgment because we knew he was a very accomplished technician and doctor.

When Daddy became sick, Jim had been asked to read his CAT scan. The morning after reading the scan, he called Todd and asked him if we could meet with him so we could talk. Todd picked me up from work during my lunch break, and we drove to the Country

Club where he was about to have lunch. As we drove in, I saw him standing by his car; sadness covered his face.

Todd let the window down on the driver's side as we drove up to him. Jim walked up to the truck and stood by the window. He and Todd always joked around but on that day he wasn't smiling. He spoke in a very serious tone.

He glanced over at me and said, "Debbie, the one thing I hate about working in a small town is that I know everybody, and it is so hard for me to give bad news to people I know personally." I nodded politely. "I've looked at your dad's scans, and I hate to say it, but it's not good. There are spots everywhere. He has spots all in his lungs and in his liver. It looks like he has cancer that has metastasized."

"Do those spots have to be cancer? Couldn't there be some other reason for them?"

"I've been doing this a long time, and I wish I could say that there might be some other explanation, but I just don't think so. It looks very bad."

Todd jumped into the conversation. "Jim, do you think he can be treated?"

"I know Dr. Cox is going to get him on the best possible treatment plan, but I'm going to be honest. The scan would indicate that your daddy only has about three months to live. Debbie, I know your parents just left Dr. Cox's office, so you might want to go to their house so you can be there for them. I'm so sorry to be the one to have to tell you this."

I nodded and tried to thank him, but the words just wouldn't come out. I buried my face in my hands and cried. Todd saw me struggling, so he spoke up instead, "Thanks, Jim. I appreciate you meeting with us and telling us in person."

I had felt this type of grief only once before—when my sister, Kathy, was shot and killed. I was only seventeen, and her life ended with such sudden violence that I was not prepared at all for her loss. I fell to my knees screaming in our den and grabbed hold of the end table beside the couch, wanting to rip the wood into pieces. I found it very difficult to control the rage, the grief, and all the emotions in between.

As an adult, I understood grief better, but I still had trouble wrapping my mind around the fact that I was about to lose my daddy. How could I accept losing the man who had always been there for me, the one who helped me with every problem I ever faced?

When Kathy died, I wished I could rewind time and spend at least a few more weeks with her to tell her how much I loved her. As with my grandmother, I kept trying to remind myself that I still had a few months to prepare for his death, but that wasn't much comfort.

We went straight to their house, the door to the house was open, and when we walked inside Mother and Daddy were both sitting in the den just staring straight ahead.

"Jim told us about your scan, Daddy."

He looked up at me with sadness in his eyes: "Yes, it wasn't really what we wanted to hear."

Todd and I sat down and joined them in their silence.

"I'm not scared of dying." He looked straight at us and said the words again, "I'm not scared of dying."

He had great faith in the Lord and God's promise of eternal life, but that didn't make any of it easier to cope with.

"Dr. Cox is getting us an appointment in Houston at M.D. Anderson," Mama said. "I hope he can get it soon."

We talked about the logistics of getting Daddy to Houston, and then we left so we could give them some time alone. When we arrived back at the house, I sat down on the couch and shook my head in complete defiant denial.

"No, Lord, there has to be some other explanation for the spots on the scan."

Even though I knew I had never known Jim to be wrong about a diagnosis, I really wanted him to get it wrong this time. I didn't want to believe he was right in Daddy's case. I took out my laptop and started researching "spots in lungs and liver." Even though the first thing that popped up on every search was "cancer," I chose to look for the obscure possibilities. I was desperate to find some glimmer of hope, but Jim was right on target with his diagnosis. Almost three months to the day that he delivered the unwanted news, my daddy went to be with the Lord.

Now almost ten years later, I was about to hear Jim give another diagnosis from a scan, but this time it would be my own. I knew he would be honest and upfront with us, and I was praying that he would see something that would give us some hope.

The sun was slowly sinking below the treetops as we drove into Jim's driveway, and as I stared at the beauty of God's creation while walking up the sidewalk to his home, I wondered how many more sunsets I would be seeing. Jim greeted us at the door and invited us inside.

After a few minutes of casual conversation, he took us past the den to an office at the back of the house. As he turned on his computer imaging system, Todd handed him the film we had received from the hospital, and he sat down at his desk to insert the disc.

We stood there motionless while Jim pulled up the pictures on the screen and looked at the scans. He put his hand underneath his chin, studying the pictures for several minutes, and then he wheeled his chair around to look at us.

He stared at us a few seconds and then he said in a soft tone, "I'm sorry Debbie. I hate to say it, but I think Dr. Cox's diagnosis is right." He went on to describe in detail the tumors in my kidney and adrenal gland.

"What type of symptoms are you having, Debbie?"

"I've had some problems with my bladder, night sweats, and I've lost a little weight, too, because I haven't had much of an appetite."

"I hate saying this, but those symptoms all point toward cancer."

The small glimmer of hope that I had been holding on to with all my might released at that very moment. I felt so defeated. But then he added, "I will say this, Debbie. The tumors look contained. That's good news."

I smiled up at Jim feeling sorry for putting him in the position of having to once again be the bearer of bad news for my family.

"Jim, I know this wasn't easy for you. Thank you for taking the time to look at it."

"I'm sorry. I wish I could have given you better news. Let me know if there is anything else I can do for you."

His words echoed what he said in that parking lot while discussing Daddy's scans. I had done everything I could think of on my own to acquire a tiny bit of hope about my situation, but instead of hope, I only found despair. At that moment I remembered what I used to hear as a little girl in church from one of our older deacons. He would say, "It's sad to say but when all hope seems gone, that's when we decide we need to call upon the Lord."

When we got home, I walked around the pool, and sat down on a lounge chair. I looked up in the heavens, and all I saw was blackness much like the darkness I felt in my heart. All of my hope, at least from the doctors, disappeared. I bowed my head, and through tears I called upon the Lord who became my only hope.

"God, please help me to accept your will even though I don't understand it. I didn't understand why Daddy had to leave this earth, and now I don't understand why this is happening to me. Help me remember that I don't have to understand anything. Remind me that you are all I need, and with you I can face

tomorrow knowing that you will never leave me nor forsake me. Help me put my hope in you and nothing else. Strengthen my faith, Lord, so I can trust you no matter where this new journey in my life will lead."

Chapter 6

SINKING IN DESPAIR

"*Had the cancer spread? Would I have to have chemotherapy and radiation treatments like Mama had to endure, or would it be too late to even fight the cancer like Daddy?*" In a few weeks, I would have my appointment in Houston and get the answers. Until then, I searched online for information about kidney cancer every night. The more I read, the more I worried. The sites all stated the same thing: other than removing the kidney, no other treatments had been found to be effective—no radiation—no chemotherapy. If it had spread, it would be fatal.

During that time of waiting, I tried to live by faith, but it was not easy. Some days I would feel so close to God, at peace in His presence knowing He would be with me through every single day and hour of my journey. On those days, I read His word, His promises. I meditated on them and praised Him for those words. Other days, I focused on the fact that I had a cancerous tumor growing inside of me. That thought coupled with the doomsday websites led me into depression.

Each day as I traveled from school to school to observe and coach new teachers, I tried to keep my mind focused on God, even talking aloud to Him during my depression: *"God, I just clawed my way up the mountain of finding Kathy's killer, and now I'm tumbling down to an even lower valley—one where I don't see any mountains tops, not even in the distance."*

My mind often drifted from talking to God to remembering Mother's cancer treatments over twenty years earlier. After several rounds of chemotherapy, she lost her hair little by little. It was one of the side effects she had feared the most, so I went with her in search of a wig that would help her cope with the loss. At one boutique, the owners found her a wig that matched her beautiful auburn-red hair.

"Let's move over to this vanity, so you can see how it looks."

Mama sat down in a chair in front of a tall mirror. As the owner helped her put the wig in place she asked, "Do you mind if I ask you a personal question?"

"No, not at all," Mama said.

"I'm doing my own informal survey with the women who come in my shop. I'm wondering—and you don't have to answer this, but before you were diagnosed with cancer, did you experience a tragedy or a difficult time in your life?"

Mother said, "Yes, as a matter of fact, my family suffered a horrible tragedy just two years ago. My oldest daughter was murdered."

"Oh—I see. I'm so sorry," the owner said, looking at Mama's eyes in the mirror. "I'm finding that almost all of the women who come in here suffered some type of trauma just a few years before their diagnosis."

I replayed that conversation in my mind and realized, *"That's why I have cancer. It's because of the emotional trauma I went through reopening Kathy's unsolved case. Over four years of intense research and drama with the police, investigators, waiting, lost evidence, district attorneys, more waiting, and the ordeal of the trial must have taken a toll on my body, and now I am destined to go down the same path as my mother."*

With all of those reminders of how difficult cancer can be, some days were harder than others to keep my eyes focused on having faith in God to see me through. Those were days that I felt like Peter did during the great storm on the Sea of Galilee, which is told in the book of Matthew:[2]

> Immediately after this, Jesus insisted that his disciples get back into the boat and cross to the other side of the lake, while he sent the people home. After sending them home, he went up into the hills by himself to pray. Night fell while he was there alone. Meanwhile, the disciples were in trouble far away from land, for a strong wind had risen, and they were fighting heavy waves.

I sat in the dark, scared of the unknown in my own ship christened *Cancer*, as if my savior wasn't in the same ship with me. And, like Peter, it seemed as though I kept getting drenched with huge waves of despair.

> About three o'clock in the morning Jesus came toward them, walking on the water. When the disciples saw him walking on the water, they were terrified. In their fear, they cried out, "It's a ghost!" But Jesus spoke to them at once. "Don't be afraid," he said. "Take courage. I am here!"

Peter and the others were afraid of the violent rain, wind and waves, just like I was afraid of the tumors, pain, and impending death.

> Then Peter called to him, "Lord, if it's really you, tell me to come to you, walking on the water." "Yes, come," Jesus said. So Peter went over the side of the boat and walked on the water toward Jesus. But when he saw the strong wind and the waves, he was terrified and began to sink. "Save me, Lord!" he shouted.

I cried out to God, too, asking Him to save me from the wretched disease that took the lives of so many I loved, and I wanted to forget about my fear and trust Him, but I found myself sinking into discouragement.

> Jesus immediately reached out and grabbed him. "You have so little faith," Jesus said. "Why did you doubt me?" When they climbed back into the boat, the wind stopped. Then the disciples worshiped him. "You really are the Son of God!" they exclaimed.

Peter stepped out of the boat with a faith that safely hovered him above the water as he walked toward Jesus. As long as he kept his eyes on his Master, Peter stayed above water; but the minute he took his focus off his Lord, he started sinking. While we waited to go to Houston, some days, my eyes stayed fixed on God. I could think, work, and function normally. But so many other days I would glance away from Him, and my faith wavered. On those days, I sank back down into my sea of desperate self-absorption.

One Wednesday, I had one of those days of discouragement. I told Todd that I really didn't feel like going to the prayer meeting at church that night. Secretly, I just wanted to sit at home, feel sorry for myself, and have my own little private pity party.

"You really need to go, Debbie. It will make you feel better."

"I just don't think I can handle going tonight. I know everyone will be asking questions about our trip to Houston—questions I don't feel like answering."

"Come on. Let's go. I'll answer all the questions."

I knew he was right. If I wanted to make it through the days ahead, I needed the prayers from my church family and their encouragement.

When we arrived at the church, Brother Cal walked across the parking lot to the fellowship hall where our prayer services were held. He saw us and came over to meet us at the car.

Sinking in Despair

"Hey, it's good to see you." He reached over for a hug. "Are you doing ok?"

"I'm doing fine."

"I want you to know I am in constant prayer for you."

"I really appreciate that, Brother Cal."

Todd shook his hand to greet him and said, "Brother Cal, I want to ask you something."

"Sure, anything. Is there something that you need? What is it? You know I will do anything to help."

"What do you think about having a special prayer service for Debbie? In the Bible it says when someone is sick to call on the elders of the church and pray over that person."

"I think it's a great idea. We've never had a prayer service for a specific person that I can remember, but I think it is a wonderful thought. Let's even open it up to the community. I know there will be others who would want to come and pray for Debbie." Glancing at me, he continued, "We'll pray specifically for healing and for strength for your family. We just had two prayer benches donated to the church, and we can use them for the first time that night. We'll have the service before you go to Houston."

He smiled at me, and I was glad I had decided to

attend the services. His sermon that night focused on how God is able—able to answer all of our prayers, that God has a plan for each and every one of us and He knows what is best for us, so sometimes His answer to our prayer is "yes," sometimes it is "no," and sometimes his answer may not be an immediate one. We might have to "wait" on that answer. I had been taught that since my childhood, yet I found myself praying, *"God, what will your answer to my prayer be? Please let it be yes, Lord."*

Listening to Brother Cal, I began to think about the many miracles recorded in the Bible—times when He said yes to those who wanted his healing touch, such as the man who was blind since birth whom God gave sight to, and the man who had been paralyzed his entire life who got up and walked. Jesus healed ten men who had leprosy and even brought Lazarus back to life after four days in the tomb. I knew God was able, and I prayed that He would heal me just as He had healed those I read about in His word. Then I began to think, *"What if it's not His will that He heal me? What if His will is for me to leave this earth? Should I be praying for His will or for what I want His will to be?"*

After the service, I went up to Brother Cal and

asked, "Do you think it's wrong for me to ask God to heal me? Should I just ask for His will to be done?"

He smiled and said, "I am praying for your healing, and I think you should do the same."

I arrived home that night reassured that God is able to do all things. I went into the kitchen and took a sheet of paper and a marker out of the desk drawer and wrote the words, "God is able. Sometimes he says "yes," "no," or "wait." I taped that piece of paper to the mirror in my bathroom so I could see it every morning when I woke up and every night as I got ready for bed. I wanted to be reminded that He is able to do anything. He is God. I was praying that this time He would say, "Yes," but I would accept any answer He gave.

※

I HAD ALREADY learned how to accept a "no" answer from God. After my mother's first lump in her breast, I begged God to let it be anything but cancer. After the second lump, I cried out to God for there to be some other explanation other than cancer. When she told me that her cancer had returned, I was so angry at God. I had already experienced too much death in my life at such a young age. My sister had been killed when I was in high school, and now, two years later, I didn't want to lose my mother. I screamed at God asking him, *"Why me, God? Why my family? Haven't we been through enough? We love you, Lord, and try to do your will in everything we do. Why would you allow this to happen to my family?"*

In my heart, I knew God didn't cause Mother's cancer, but he might have allowed it to happen and that made me even angrier. Yet, I also knew He might use her sickness for some purpose that I might never understand. After all, He was in control—not me. I needed God to be with me through this difficult trial because He was my source of strength through every battle I would ever face during my lifetime—not me.

Mother beat her cancer for the second time, and the Lord used her strong faith to draw others to Him through her ordeal. She played the piano for the church each Sunday even though her body was weary from the chemotherapy and radiation. She counseled with others who were going through the fight with cancer telling them to never give up hope and depend on the Lord. As I saw God work in and through Mama, my faith in His abilities to work all things for good strengthened. That growth in my faith laid the foundation I needed for my own fight with the disease.

Sinking in Despair

༄

SINCE CHILDHOOD, SINGING in the choir has been how I express my worship to God; it is my great joy to sing up to Him and I look forward to it every Sunday, except that coming one. I didn't think I could sing praises to God in my depressed state—*what kind of worship would that be?* I thought. Yet, one by one, the choir members reached out to tell me how they were praying for my healing and strength. My spirit improved, and I kept reminding myself of God's glorious promise. He never promised healing, but He did promise eternal life for those who accept God's gracious gift, Jesus. At a young age, I did that—I accepted Jesus' sacrifice for me and promised to make Him my Lord. Because of the promise I made to God and He made to me, I always had a song in my heart even when the problems of life were overwhelming. It's just that sometimes during my despair, I shut the door to my heart from him, so I couldn't hear the praises.

My eyes met with the announcements for the service in the bulletin—a special prayer service would be held in the church sanctuary for me, and all friends and church members were invited to attend. The door to my joyful song had opened wide. I felt so thankful and humbled for the spiritual support. Yet, I have always been a very shy person and the thought of a service just for me also made me feel a little anxious.

My shyness was pretty painful as a child. I remember the Sunday morning I asked Jesus to be my Lord and Savior. I knew if I wanted to make a public decision, it would mean that I would have to walk all the way down the aisle to the front of the church with a lot of people watching me. I held the pew so tightly, my knuckles turned white. When I finally let go and started walking to meet the pastor, I no longer cared who was looking at me. I knew I was a sinner. I needed a Savior—period. The burden of my sins seemed to be lifted away with each step until I felt weightless at the altar.

At this time in my life, I still didn't like being the center of attention, but I knew the power of prayer and I wanted to be healed. A prayer service just for me meant that the call on God to heal me would be multiplied with many voices rising up to Him. Although I didn't make it known, I desperately wanted that powerful plea to go into the heavens, and I knew it fit into God's will. Jesus even told his disciples a story about how God hears us when we continually come before him with our needs:

> "There was a city judge," he said, "a very godless man who had great contempt for everyone. A widow of that city came to him frequently to appeal for justice against a man who had harmed her. The judge ignored her for a while, but eventually she got on his nerves. 'I fear neither God nor man,' he said to himself, 'but this woman bothers me. I'm going to see that she gets justice, for she is wearing me out with her constant coming!'" Then the Lord said, "If even an evil judge can be worn down like that, don't you think that God will surely give justice to his people who plead with him day and night? Yes! He will answer them quickly! (Luke 18:2–8)

That was my prayer—that He would hear my constant plea and the pleas of others as we asked for my healing. It comforted me greatly to know that God expects constant prayer and that He would be there with us as we prayed, as Jesus promised when he said, "Where two or three gather together as my followers, I am there among them."[3]

Chapter 7

THE POWER OF PRAYER

When the night of the service arrived, I didn't really know what to expect. As we walked into the church, Todd, Brittany, Katelyn, and I walked down to the front where Brother Cal motioned for us to sit. He started the service with a prayer asking God to forgive any sins that any of us might have in our lives that would hinder our prayers from being heard by the Lord.

While everyone silently searched their hearts and prayed for forgiveness, a holy silence filled the room like that mentioned in the Bible during the battle of Jericho. God told the soldiers to walk around the walls of the city seven times without uttering a sound. I'm sure it seemed like a strange command for an army to march in silence, but at the end of the silence came the battle cry of victory. I was praying that at the end of our cries to the Lord, I would have victory in my battle as well.

After several minutes, Brother Cal asked Todd and me to come and kneel down on a small prayer bench. One by one, those who filled the pews came by and laid their hands on us and prayed that God would heal my body and take away the cancer. I stayed on my knees with my head bowed and eyes closed as my family and friends walked by and leaned over me, touching my head or shoulders as they prayed aloud.

"Debbie, your family has meant so much to me over the years. I had to come and pray for you because I love all of you so much."

I knew the voice immediately. It was Jeremy, my brother's best friend growing up. He told me how grateful he was for the Christian influence my family had been to him. Then he and his wife prayed that God would heal me and restore my health.

Tears fell, the first of many I would shed that night.

"God, we know you hold this precious lady in your hands, and you are the divine healer. We ask that you heal her completely. Give her more time on this earth to serve you. We know there is nothing impossible for you, oh Lord."

The sweet voice whispering in my ear was one of our oldest and most faithful servants to the church.

"We are asking that you take away her cancer, comfort her, and give her strength to make the journey to Houston. Be with the doctors and guide their hands as they operate. Send her back to us whole and healthy, Lord."

After she prayed, I thought of so many in our church who had lived their lives through good times and bad depending on God at all times. I wanted to one day be the voice of an older, godly woman, to be able to pray for others and serve in the church like she had done for so many years. In my inner spirit, I begged God to hear her prayers as well as all the others said on my behalf that night.

There were over a hundred friends and family who came that night to pray for my healing. Some of them fasted for days before the service. It was an indescribable night. They all poured out their hearts to God on behalf of my family and me. I was overwhelmed by the love and support of my church family and all of my friends who had come to the service. When everyone had finished praying, it was so quiet and peaceful. I knew the Lord had been present among us during that time. I knew that He heard our prayers.

When I got home, I went straight to my bedroom where I could be alone to talk to God.

I knelt as I had done at the church, but this time I placed my folded hands on the bed as if I were a child again about to say my nighttime prayers. Every night, Mama or Daddy would come to my room, and I would say the same prayer, as my own girls did: *"Now I lay me down to sleep. I pray the Lord my soul to keep. Guide me safely through the night, and wake me with the morning light."*

(Picture of girls saying prayers when they were little)

I didn't need to pray for the Lord to keep my soul any more. I knew without a shadow of a doubt that the day I asked him to be my Lord and Savior and repented of my sins, He had done just as He promised, and my soul would forever be kept in His hand. He had taken me into His family and adopted me as His own child. Instead, I wanted to pray that He would guide me safely through the many nights to come and allow me to wake to many more mornings. I wanted to live. I poured out my heart to Him.

"God, you heard the prayers of so many tonight. Please, now hear my own prayer. Take this cancer away from me. I know you are the great physician, and it doesn't matter what any other physician says. You can take it away just by saying the words—Just like you spoke the world and all that is within it into existence. Please heal my body and continue to heal my relationship with you. Give me the faith that I need to believe you can heal me."

After my prayer, I sat on the side of the bed and picked up my Bible from the nightstand beside me. As I held it in my hands, I prayed that God would show me a verse to comfort my soul—a different verse from the one He gave me on the bathroom floor in Daddy's hotel room in Houston.

I opened the Bible and looked down at the page. I gasped. My heart leaped. I stared at the Scripture for several minutes as if I were in a trance. I was very familiar with this passage; I had even played the part of the woman during an Easter play at church. I read verses 25–34 of Mark chapter 5 again, as if it were brand new:

> "In the crowd was a woman who had been sick for twelve years with a hemorrhage. She had suffered much from many doctors through the years and had become poor from paying them, and was no better but, in fact, was worse."

She was just a character in a play before, but now I could completely identify with her.

> "She had heard all about the wonderful miracles Jesus did, and that is why she came up behind him through the crowd and touched his clothes. For she thought to herself, "If I can just touch his clothing, I will be healed."

Those were my thoughts too. I had been taught as a child about the many healings Jesus performed during His life on earth. As an adult, with many years of learning about and knowing Him as my personal Savior, I knew it was within His mighty power to heal me.

And sure enough, as soon as she had touched him, the bleeding stopped and she knew she was well! Jesus realized at once that healing power had gone out from him, so He turned around in the crowd and asked, "Who touched my clothes?" His disciples said to him, "all this crowd pressing around you and you ask who touched you?" But he kept on looking around to see who it was who had done it. Then the frightened woman, trembling at the realization of what had happened to her, came and fell at His feet and told him what she had done. And he said to her, "Daughter, your faith has made you well; go in peace, healed of your disease."

When the woman touched Jesus because of her need, He called her out of the crowd. She trembled and fell to her knees because she knew she had been healed by the Savior. *"Lord,"* I cried out. *"I'm on my knees now, seeking that same healing, and I will love you whether You heal me or not."*

I revisited that Easter play as if I were looking down on myself as a middle-aged wife and mother once again dressed in a blue robe with a cream scarf draped around my head and shoulders, kneeling down to touch the hem of Jesus' garment. I sang out in joyful praise:

> My Jesus, My Savior,
> Lord there is no one like you,
> All of my days, I want to praise
> The wonders of Your mighty love.
>
> My comfort, my shelter,
> Tower of refuge and strength
> Let every breath, all that I am
> Never cease to worship You.
>
> Shout to the Lord, all the earth let us sing,
> Power and majesty, praise to the King!
> Mountains bow down and the seas will roar,
> At the sound of your name!
> I sing for joy at the work of your hands,
> Forever I'll love you, forever I'll stand
> Nothing compares to the promise I have in You.[4]

My heart rejoiced because of what God revealed to me that night. Instead of comforting me with words about how He'd be with me as I walked through the valley of the shadow of death, the word for me now was that through faith, He could perform miracles. I scanned the narrative of the woman and Jesus again, closed my Bible, and laid it back on the nightstand.

Your faith has made you well. Your faith has made you well. The words kept cycling from my mind down into my heart and through my spirit as I closed my eyes and imagined myself rising up to the Savior to touch the hem of His garment. When I opened my eyes, I felt a peace and calmness that surpassed even the serenity at the prayer meeting.

Chapter 8

THE WAITING

I WAITED OVER HALF my lifetime to find the man who killed my older sister, so I should have been more comfortable with waiting now. This was different. I saw Daddy's symptoms grow worse by the day, and in three short months he was gone. It had only been a short time since my diagnosis, and I knew that every second counted. While God had given me a peace and assurance of His healing touch, I still battled with fear on a daily basis.

I tried to stay strong in what I knew to be true about God and my faith, but it was a constant struggle. Whenever I took my thoughts off of Jesus and onto dying before my children were grown, a wave of panic would rise up and pin me down. I couldn't breathe. But even then, God knew how to comfort me.

"Mama, I have something for you," Brittany softly said walking into my room. "I wrote you a letter that I want you to take with you to Houston." She reached out her hand and gave me a folded paper.

"Can I read it now?"

"Sure."

I carefully unfolded the paper as if it were a specially wrapped present. Even though Brittany's handwriting was barely legible because of her dysgraphia, a writing disorder, her thoughtfulness and love came through every stroke of the pen:

> *Dear Mama,*
>
> *I continually think about you. I love you so much. I know God has made you strong. Wherever you are, whatever you go through, don't ever fret because God carries you. Your dad is very proud of your strength right now. Don't worry.*
>
> *Love,*
> *Brittany*

I smiled and reached out to hug her; we held each other tightly.

The Waiting

Dear mama,

i continually think about you. i will miss you. I love you soo much. Please know i think of you every minute. God will carry you. i know God has made you strong. your Dad is very proud right now. Don't worry

Love, Brittany

Whereever you are
whatever you go through
Don't ever fret
Because God carries you.

"I will keep it in my Bible and read it every night to give me even more strength. Thank you, Britt."

Katelyn walked in the room and hopped up on the bed. "What's that?" she asked, pointing to the paper in my hand.

"It's a letter Brittany wrote to me."

"Can I read it?"

I handed it to her. She read it and smiled.

"I'm praying for you, too, Mama. You can handle anything."

"You both know how much I love you, right? I know I've told you this before, but I'm going to say it again. No matter how this turns out, I want you to know that I'm going to be ok. I know God is with me." I smiled to reassure them that I meant those words. They tried to hide their fears from me, but their worry was so intense that I could see it shining through their eyes.

Chapter 9

A JOURNEY FOR ANSWERS

TODD AND I decided to go to Houston alone. We thought it would be better for the girls to stay at home and attend school so their lives would be as normal as possible instead of riding the rollercoaster of emotions we were about to strap ourselves into.

Throughout the six and a half hour drive, I knew that God was with me and I could lean on Him no matter what came my way and that gave me peace, but the reality of waiting for test results and the physical pain I might have to suffer like my daddy scared me.

I was familiar enough with the Bible to know that God has a solution or reason for every fear, so I considered how Jesus dealt with these same complex emotions as He faced the end of His own life on earth. Shortly before His death, He went to the Garden of

Gethsemane to pray. The One who existed before the creation of the earth told His disciples that His soul was crushed by sorrow. Even though He was God, He was also a man who would suffer the real pain of a cruel death on the cross; and even worse than that, He knew He would soon be weighed down with the sins of the world on His own soul.

Jesus fell to the ground and asked our Father to take the cup of suffering away from Him if there were any other way to accomplish His purpose. He prayed for deliverance from the pain, but ultimately, that God's will and not His own would take place. I knew I would accept God's will for my life, too, even if that included the pain and suffering of dying from cancer, but until He revealed His plan for me, I would continue to pray for my healing.

I guess Todd could sense my somber mood, so he played the CD of our new choir music. The first song, "Even In the Valley," said everything my heart couldn't:

> High upon this mountain,
> the sun is shining bright
> My heart is filled with gladness,
> here above the cares of life
> But I've just come through the valley,
> of trouble, fear and pain

It was there I came to know my God,
enough to stand and say
Even in the valley, God is good
Even in the valley, He is faithful and true
He carries His children through,
like He said He would
Even in the valley, God is good

This road of life has led you,
to a valley of defeat,
You wonder if the father,
has heard your desperate plea
There is hope in that rugged place,
where tears of sorrow dwell
Can't you hear Him gently whispering,
"I'm here and all is well."
Even in the valley, God is good
Even in the valley, He is faithful and true
He carries His children through,
like He said He would
Even in the valley, God is good.[5]

As I listened to the words repeated over and over that even in the valley God is good, I turned my head to the window and warm tears flowed down my cheeks. I knew the words were so true. God was good, and in my valley of despair, He heard me and was near to me. He remained good through the good times in my life and even in the bad times.

I stared out the window watching the beautiful grassy hills adorned with tiny, wild flowers slowly become dry, flat land with trees that dwarfed the tall pines and oaks of home. The change was subtle, taking hours to complete. It reminded me of the subtleness of my cancer invasion, and I started to think of all I could have done: *"Why didn't I go to the doctor sooner? Why did I wait so long? If I had gone as soon as I experienced the first symptoms, the cancer might have been contained in the kidney instead of spreading to the adrenal gland."*

Glancing back at the rustic beauty of the pastureland where hundreds of cattle grazed, I reminded myself of God's promise that he would never leave me nor forsake me. Even though I was fearful of what the girls and Todd might go through if cancer took my life and the pain I might suffer, I could say for certain I did not fear death. The first Bible verse I learned as a child gave me that assurance: "For God so loved the world, that He gave His only Son, that whoever believes in Him should not perish but have eternal life."[6] I knew beyond a shadow of a doubt that if I died, my life on earth would be over, but my life after death would begin. I closed my eyes and tried to focus on that promise as I fell asleep listening to the words of the song.

When we arrived in Houston, Todd and I checked into the same hotel where I had stayed with Mama and Daddy. Walking into the beautiful lobby brought back memories of the doctor's visit, the long walk across the sky bridge, and the outpouring of distress in the dark bathroom. Yet, I also remembered my daddy's courage, strength, and enduring faith even in the grief.

That night, we called the girls to tell them we had arrived at the hotel. I didn't want them to be upset so I tried to stay strong, just like I had seen my father stay strong for us.

"Katelyn, how is everything going?"

"It's fine, Mama. I did really well on my test today in math."

"That's great, baby. What's Brittany doing?"

"She's in the den with Grandmama watching TV."

"Well, I just wanted you to know we made it to the hotel, and your daddy will call you as soon as we finish with all my appointments tomorrow. Don't stay up too late tonight."

"We won't. I love you, Mama."

"I love you too. Do you want to speak to Brittany?

"Is she close by?"

"She's right here beside me."

"Hey, Mama."

"Hey, Britt."

"Are you ok? Are you worried, Mama?"

"No, I'm fine. When I start getting worried, I just pull out the letter you wrote to me, and it calms my fears. Now you and Katelyn need to go on to bed so you won't be tired for school in the morning. Tell your grandmama I said hello, and we will call you tomorrow after my tests are done. I love you. Good night."

"Good night, Mama."

❧

THE NEXT MORNING Todd and I walked across the sky bridge. I had been sent a letter from the hospital with a detailed schedule for the day. Yellow, green, and red lines on the floor were supposed to help me navigate to my destinations, but being navigationally challenged, I was glad that Todd had his bearings well fitted and could help me find my way.

"Do you need the map they sent to me to help find my first appointment?" I asked.

"I looked at it last night, and I think I know where we need to go."

We passed by a small cafeteria on the first floor. "Do you want to get some breakfast before your first appointment? I think we have time."

"I'm not really hungry, and I better not eat since they will be doing a lot of tests today. They didn't tell me I couldn't eat in the letter, but I don't want to take a chance and have to come back later. You go ahead and get something though because it's probably going to be a long day. I don't mind sitting with you while you eat."

"I'll just wait until you can eat with me."

We walked on down to a set of elevators and then started down a long hallway. My itinerary included having blood work done, a CAT scan, and then an appointment with a kidney specialist, Dr. Martin, who would be my doctor. We followed one of the colored lines to the lab where I would have my blood drawn. The hospital was so efficient that it didn't take long, and then we began looking for my next appointment in radiology.

When I walked into the area for my CAT scan, several rows of people, young and old were drinking bottles of the chalky contrast required before the CAT scans could be performed. I looked around thinking about how they all had their own stories of how cancer had invaded their lives and put them on a different course for their future. I wondered how many of them had the comforting presence of the Lord to help them with their journey. I knew in my heart that the only way I was able to cope with what was happening in my life was because of my relationship with Christ. The sight of it reminded me of what Daddy said when he was going through his testing.

"I feel like I'm being herded like cattle into these testing rooms."

We laughed, but it was so sad to see so many people sick and hurting. When I looked around in the waiting room, I thought his description still fit.

All the tests that were done previously had to be redone at M.D. Anderson with their top-notch equipment, and they wanted their own radiologist to read the tests. This time, when I had the CAT scan done, I no longer feared the unknown. Now I was just determined to get everything done, so I could begin the process of getting well.

Once I completed all of my tests, we followed the yellow path to Dr. Martin's office, where we signed in at the nurses' station, sat down in the waiting room, and waited for our turn to see him. I flipped through several magazines that were lying on the table in front of me, and as I looked at the purses and the clothes that were being advertised, I thought about how I would have been really interested in those things just a few months earlier. Now none of them seemed important. With just a few words, "You have cancer," my priorities in life changed. Things don't last forever—even good health doesn't last forever.

I remembered Daddy reminded us during his final days of that very thing. He wanted Mother to move into a smaller house so she wouldn't have to worry about the upkeep of a larger home. Mother didn't want to even talk about it.

"Lee Roy, I can't leave that house," she told him. You built it, and it has all of the things we have worked for all these years."

"They are just things, Precious. It's just stuff. Those things won't matter in the end. They are not eternal."

He had a firm grasp on the importance of faith instead of worldly possessions, and in his final days, he wanted all of us to understand that concept. In the weeks ahead I would have to come to grips with it more and more.

When I was called to the back, a nurse checked my vital signs and escorted me into a room. Todd sat down in a chair by a desk while I climbed up and sat on the observation bed. After a few minutes, a middle-aged man with short dark hair walked in and smiled as he stuck out his hand to greet us.

"Good morning, Mrs. Wilson. I'm Dr. Martin. How are you today?" He had a heavy Middle Eastern accent, but I could understand his English perfectly.

"I could be better, I guess," and I smiled at him as he moved closer to us. Todd and I both shook his hand, and I took a deep breath as he pulled up my CAT scan report on his computer and began discussing the test results. He read the radiologist's report to us first.

"It is confirmed, Mrs. Wilson that you have a large tumor in your right kidney and in the adrenal gland right above it. Did you know you are also borderline anemic?" I didn't know that but thought it was irrelevant at that point. He continued, "I have read your report from Dr. Cox, and he indicated that you have been experiencing fatigue, night sweats, and weight loss. He even stated that you have had some severe bladder problems. Surprisingly I do not believe the bladder symptoms you were experiencing were associated with the tumors you have. I do feel that you are fortunate that the symptoms with your bladder began to show up, though, because in time the tumors would have spread outside the kidney and adrenal gland and metastasized."

I smiled at him because I knew it wasn't luck. It was the Lord watching over me. Maybe this was part of God's plan in healing me of this disease. Maybe I had caught the cancer in time to be healed.

He handed me a copy of the radiology report, and I glanced down the page: *"The tumor represents the patient's known renal cell cancer."* The diagnosis of cancer had always been my nightmare, my biggest fear, and there it was in black and white—the same diagnosis from another radiologist.

I glanced back up at the doctor as he said, "The tumors appear to be contained, which is good news. If the tumor in the kidney were smaller, I would consider taking out only part of the kidney, but due to the size and location I feel that the best course of action would be a nephrectomy, which is a complete removal of the kidney. We will also want to remove the entire adrenal gland."

"Are you sure the tumor is malignant?"

"Based on my experience, I would have to say that I do believe it is malignant. The radiologist also agrees with that diagnosis."

"Will you be doing a biopsy to determine if it is malignant before the surgery?"

"There is really no need to do a biopsy first because

the tumors must be removed regardless, and the only way to do that is to remove the organs. But we will analyze them after they are removed."

"When can we do it?"

"I'll have my assistant give you a call and schedule the surgery."

Even though I was pretty sure I knew the answer to the next question, I asked anyway, "Will I have to have any radiation or chemotherapy after the surgery?"

"Kidney cancer is one of the few types of cancer that does not respond to those types of treatments. The treatment for kidney cancer is to remove the tumors. I believe your prognosis is very good. Now, do you enjoy eating steak?"

"Yes, I do."

"Good, because it will help if you eat quite a few between now and the time of your surgery to help with the anemia."

I smiled, "That won't be difficult."

He patted me on the shoulder and said, "Is there anything else you want to ask or discuss?"

"There's just one more thing. I am very anxious to do this surgery. Is there any way we could schedule it for today?"

"Well, today might be a little soon," he said smiling,

"but I promise we will try to get it scheduled as soon as possible."

When we left the office, Todd and I walked across the sky bridge and went in the hotel restaurant. As I stared at the menu I remembered Dr. Martin's request and ordered filet mignon. Todd ordered a steak too, but when our food arrived we both just stared at our plates.

"You aren't eating. You need to eat."

"You aren't eating either, I said as I glanced over at his plate."

"I just wish we could go back in time, and this never would have happened. I'm scared, and I don't want to have surgery."

"Everything is going to be ok. I promise."

Todd smiled at me, and after more prodding from him, I ate several bites of steak even though I really didn't have an appetite.

After supper we went back to the hotel room, and retrieved the message waiting for us on the phone.

"Mrs. Wilson, this is Christina, Dr. Martin's nurse. We have scheduled your surgery for the day after tomorrow." She continued with instructions for me to follow, but I had to bow my head and thank God that I wouldn't have to wait much longer for the surgery.

That night before going to sleep, I opened my Bible,

read a passage from the book of Hebrews that spoke of great examples of faith, and thought about how it applied to me:

> It would take too long to recount the stories of the faith of Gideon, Barak, Samson, Jephthah, David, Samuel, and all the prophets. By faith these people overthrew kingdoms, ruled with justice, and received what God had promised them. They shut the mouths of lions, quenched the flames of fire, and escaped death by the edge of the sword.

"I want to have the faith of David, Samuel, or any of the prophets because my goal is their goal—to escape death."

> Their weakness was turned to strength. They became strong in battle and put whole armies to flight. Women received their loved ones back again from death.

"I'm not strong enough to fight this battle alone, but through Your strength, I can persevere."

> But others were tortured, refusing to turn from God in order to be set free. They placed their hope in a better life after the resurrection. Some

were jeered at, and their backs were cut open with whips. Others were chained in prisons. Some died by stoning, some were sawed in half, and others were killed with the sword."[7]

"Some men and women of God experienced mighty miracles by faith and others over hundreds of years have died because of their faith, but I am praying, Lord, for healing so that I might experience a mighty miracle by faith. Like those great heroes and anointed prophets of God, having faith doesn't mean that my life will be perfect and free of suffering. But You did promise that I would be provided eternal life if I had faith—faith in You and what You did on a cross over 2,000 years ago."

I quickly turned to chapter five of Mark and read the passage again about the woman who had touched Jesus' hem and was healed because of her faith—not in any fabric but in the One person who heals physically and spiritually. I prayed for healing again that night, and fell asleep as I visualized walking up to Him through the crowd of people to touch the hem of His garment.

Chapter 10

PREPARING FOR THE BIG DAY

THE NIGHT BEFORE my surgery I sat in the bed reading over all of my instructions to prepare for the next day. During previous surgeries, I had to remove my fingernail polish so that wasn't a big surprise. I kept reading as Todd watched TV.

"You are kidding!" I shouted.

"What? What is it?"

"This says I can't wear any makeup tomorrow."

"Then I guess that means you won't be wearing any makeup."

I didn't even let Todd see me without makeup until several months after we were married. Call it a southern girl's weakness, but I have always believed that you should look your best no matter what the circumstance.

"You look beautiful with or without makeup."

"This is not going to be easy for me in more ways than one!" I ranted.

He laughed and went back to watching the TV while I went back to sulking over one more reason to dread the next day.

The hospital where I would have my surgery was a few buildings down from our motel, so we drove there the next morning before daylight. We checked in and were told to wait in an open area waiting room until my name was called. Not long after we arrived, my brother, sister, mother, Brother Cal, and a good friend from church, Mr. Owens, came walking down the hallway. I felt very blessed that they had made the trip to pray with me before going into surgery.

Mr. Owens kept us entertained with stories of his adventures when he worked for the railroad company. He even performed a magic trick that he had been practicing for the children at church. It really helped to keep my mind off of the surgery.

When my name was called, Todd and I went to a different room where we saw lots of hospital beds lined up with other patients waiting for their procedures. A nurse in blue scrubs met us at the door.

"You can change into this gown and put your clothes in this bag," she said as she handed me the

Preparing for the Big Day

bag. She pulled the curtain around us, and I started to change into the gown.

"What is this? Do you think I have to wear this net thing on my head too?"

"I guess you do. It was in the bag."

"No makeup and now this funny hat. I can't catch a break!"

Todd grinned and helped me put my clothes in the bag after I changed. Once in bed, she pulled the curtains back, and I looked across and smiled at a young woman in a bed beside me. A man held her hand as they talked quietly.

I whispered to Todd, "I guess everybody didn't get the same instructions as I got."

"What are you talking about?"

I motioned for him to look at the woman. He grinned.

"She not only has on foundation makeup, but her lipstick color is gorgeous!"

"I guess they aren't very strict about the rules."

"That would have been one piece of information I would have liked to have known."

We both laughed. It felt so good to laugh. There hadn't been much laughter in our lives since that day in September when we visited Dr. Cox. The anesthesiologist stopped by to talk to us, which meant it would soon be time to say goodbye to Todd. I started to tear up, but he bent down and kissed me on the forehead and told me he loved me, and I felt better. As soon as he stood back up, two nurses walked over to the bed and told me it was time to take a ride. I knew what that meant. I smiled at Todd and took a deep breath as they wheeled me down the hall to the operating room.

༄

When I was a little girl, I loved having my own room with pink walls and pretty pink curtains, but I hated sleeping by myself. Every night I would be frightened by what looked like bugs in the sheer curtains as the moonlight shined through my bedroom window exposing the weights sewn into the fabric to make them hang correctly. I even looked under my bed before I went to sleep to check for monsters, and hid under the covers every time I got scared of where they might be.

In the book of Job, God appeared to Job in the midst of horrific losses and disease and told him how to deal with his monsters. He made Job look into the face of a mighty serpent-like sea crocodile and said,

If you lay your hands upon him, you will long remember the battle that ensues, and you will never try it again! No, it's useless to try to capture him. It is frightening even to think about it! No one dares to stir him up, let alone try to conquer him. And if no one can stand before him, who can stand before me? I owe no one anything. Everything under the heaven is mine.[8]

God basically asked Job, *"Are you going to try to handle this monster yourself? Face the truth about the monsters in your life. You can't handle them. Give them to me. I made all of creation, and only I can handle your monsters."*

The monster I had to face was cancer, and I couldn't hide under the covers to get away from it. I had to grow up and face it like Jesus expected me to—hiding safely in my Savior's arms, letting Him comfort me so that He would give me a peace that only He could give. Wheeling down the hall to the operating room, I closed my eyes and asked Jesus to fight my monster for me.

Chapter 11

THE ROAD TO RECOVERY

"Mrs. Wilson, are you doing alright today?" a nurse asked.

"Yes, but hopefully I'll be doing much better after this is over."

She smiled and said, "We are going to take good care of you. In just a few minutes, you will be sound asleep, and when you wake up, it will be all over."

"I'm definitely ready for that!"

The anesthesiologist walked up beside my bed and said, "We are going to give you something in your IV that will help you relax."

I stared at all the equipment around me and began to feel sleepy. The room got darker and darker, until I was finally asleep. The last thing I remember is walking up to the Savior and touching the hem of His garment.

Todd and the others waited in a large room for over four hours. When the surgery was over, Dr. Martin met with Todd in a small room beside the waiting area.

"Mr. Wilson, your wife is doing fine. The procedure went very smoothly. She will have several small incisions where the laparoscopic equipment was used to remove her kidney and adrenal gland. We closed the cuts with surgical glue, so there won't be any staples or stitches to worry about. There were no complications, but we will need to check her blood again for anemia to make sure she won't need a transfusion."

"What about the cancer, Dr. Martin? Could you tell if it was contained? Did you get all of it?"

"We did not see any evidence of metastasis, but we will need to wait on the lab results to be sure."

"That's great!"

"I'll be making rounds this evening, and I'll check on her. Do you have any other questions?"

"When can I see her?"

"The nurse will come and get you in a few minutes so you can go to the recovery area and stay with her until she wakes up completely."

Todd stuck out his hand to shake Dr. Martin's hand and said, "Thank you so much, Dr. Martin. I appreciate all you have done for us."

The Road to Recovery

Todd went back to the main waiting room and told everyone the good news about my condition. Within a few minutes, a nurse escorted him to the recovery area.

When I woke up, I could feel Todd's hand on my shoulder. I moaned, "Is it over? Are they finished?"

He leaned over me and kissed my forehead. "It's over. You are fine. Everything went fine."

I smiled as I closed my eyes again and drifted back to sleep. That night I went in and out of sleep, pressing at will the pump that delivered the pain relief medication.

A nurse woke me the next morning to check my vital signs, when Dr. Martin walked in the room.

"Mrs. Wilson, how are you feeling?"

"I think I'm doing better than I was yesterday," I said with a smile.

"Everything went well with the surgery. We removed the kidney and your adrenal gland, and the tissue has been sent to the pathologist. We should get a report in a week or two. As I told your husband yesterday, there were no surprises. I believe the cancer found in the kidney and the adrenal gland was contained, but we won't know for sure until we see the report."

"That sounds very good, doctor."

"In a little while, the nurse will come and help you get out of bed because today I want you to do a little bit of walking. You can start out by walking around the nurses' station. Then you can begin walking slowly down the hallway. The more you move now, the faster you will recuperate."

I didn't want to sit up much less walk at that moment, and when he left the room I leaned back on my pillow and drifted back to sleep.

Later that afternoon when the nurse came to help me, I managed to get out of bed and walk around the nurses' station with a little help from Todd.

"You want to try one more loop around?"

"No, I don't even like to exercise when I haven't been operated on much less when I have just had my kidney removed," I said sarcastically.

The next day, I made two loops around the nurses' station, and I walked all the way down the hallway twice. I felt so much better that I even decided to put on some makeup and fix my hair. When Dr. Martin made his rounds he was surprised to see me sitting up in a chair beside the bed.

"Well, it looks like our patient is feeling much better today."

"I definitely feel more like myself."

"That's very good. I do have some good news for

you. Your blood work came back from the lab and it looked fine, so we will not have to do a transfusion."

"I guess those steaks I ate before surgery paid off," I said as I looked over at Todd and grinned.

Dr. Martin smiled and said, "Well, let's take a look at those incisions."

After making sure everything looked to his satisfaction, he wrote on my chart and said, "I'm going to let you begin eating some solid food today, and if you continue to improve I don't see why you can't go home tomorrow evening."

Even though I still felt some pain, I felt ready to go home.

"If you do leave the hospital tomorrow, you will still need to stay in Houston for a few days before you travel."

"That won't be a problem at all. We are staying at the hotel next to the hospital, and I'm sure my wonderful nurse here can take good care of me," I said as I grabbed Todd's hand.

The next day, I was discharged, relieved to have the surgery behind me and to hear from cancer specialists that they believed the cancer had not spread.

Days later as we drove back home, the level of peace that came upon me the night of the prayer service returned. I prayed that God would help me have the faith to believe that He had healed me from cancer, and I kept telling myself, *"They got it all, Debbie. Be thankful! The Lord allowed you to catch the cancer early and have it removed. It is out of your body—It is gone—You are fine."*

Chapter 12

UNEXPECTED NEWS

"Welcome Home!" read a large banner hanging above the carport that the girls made. I got out of the car holding the pillow over my stomach that I had used to soften the bumps on the ride home. Brittany and Katelyn came running around the car to the passenger's side to hug me.

"Mama, I'm so glad you're home!" shouted Katelyn.

"Me too, Mama!"

"You look so good," my brother, Steve, said walking behind me into the house.

"You know I was going to offer to give you one of my kidneys if you needed it. Amy wanted to give you one of hers, but I told her no way. I was giving you mine."

"Yeah, I bet the two of you were arguing over that,

but not about who would get to give me one. I'm sure it was about who would *have* to do it!"

"No seriously, you definitely don't look like you just had a kidney removed."

"Well, I can tell you that I feel like I just had a kidney removed."

I needed some sense of normalcy in my life again, so that night we sat in the lounge chairs by the pool and talked for quite a while. For the first time in many weeks, I no longer felt burdened by that dark cloud of gloom and doom. I no longer felt like the girls would grow up without me or that I would not enjoy the pool next summer. I wanted to believe that this new sense of life was God's way of letting me know He had performed a miracle, but I was too afraid to believe it completely. I kept reminding myself that Dr. Martin felt that the cancer was contained, but that is exactly what Mama's doctors told her, too, only to find out years later that it had spread to her other breast.

We laughed and talked until I got tired, and then we went inside for the night. It was hard to believe it had only been weeks since I had been diagnosed with cancer because it really felt like a lifetime.

Unexpected News

WHILE WAITING FOR the pathology report from Dr. Martin, I kept praying each night that it would confirm his belief that the cancer had not spread outside the walls of my kidney and adrenal gland. After a week at home, I began expecting the call, so I kept my cell phone by my side at all times. Todd was able to take off work and stay home with me while I was recuperating, and he tried his best to keep my mind off the waiting.

One morning after the girls had gone to school, Todd opened the French doors and stepped outside to talk to his brother on the phone about how I was doing. I made my way through the den and when I passed by the snack bar in the kitchen, I saw my phone. I had forgotten to take it with me to the bedroom, so I picked it up and saw that I had a voice message. I pressed play and immediately recognized the accent. It was Dr. Martin. I stepped out onto the patio to listen to the message.

"Mrs. Wilson, this is Dr. Martin. I have very good news for you. I will try to call you again later, but I wanted to let you know the results of the pathology report."

My heart skipped a beat. *"Lord, please let him tell me that my cancer was contained. Please, Lord."*

"I have good news for you. The pathology report

came back and the tumors we removed were not cancerous. Surprisingly, you do not have cancer."

I kept holding the phone to my right ear, but my left hand went straight up into the air, lifted high to the heavens, and I fell to my knees on the hard concrete. I started crying, mouthing the words, "Thank you, Lord. Thank you, God, for my miracle!" as I continued listening to the message.

Todd had turned around from talking on the phone when he heard me come out of the door, and when he saw me on the ground, he quickly hung up and came rushing over to me.

"It's not cancer! It's not cancer!" I shouted through sobs as I continued listening to the message.

He picked me up from the ground and held me.

"How do you know it isn't cancer? Was that Dr. Martin? What did he say?"

"I haven't really heard everything. I just heard that I don't have cancer."

"Put it on speaker phone and play it again."

I pressed play.

Again I heard the words, "I have good news for you. The pathology report came back and the tumors we removed were not cancerous. You do not have cancer."

I had been praying for the cancer to be contained, and God had healed me in a different way than I could have ever imagined.

"The pathology report came back, and the diagnosis is renal oncocytoma. Fortunately you have been diagnosed with this very rare condition that is usually found in men and women much older than you. I need to see you back for your post visit in a few weeks. I am out of the office traveling, but I will try to reach you again later."

I stood in shock with tears flowing down my cheeks. "I had faith that God could heal me, so why was I acting so surprised when He had done just that?" Then I remembered what happened when the woman touched the hem of Jesus' garment. After she was healed, she became frightened by the realization of what had just taken place. I was not frightened. I was in awe of His power and His majesty.

I turned and ran into the house and grabbed the house phone.

"Who are you calling?"

"Brother Cal."

I could barely contain my composure as I gave him the good news. I called Mama, Amy, and Steve while Todd went outside to call all of his family. Then we stood in the same spot in the kitchen and held each other just like we had done weeks before after receiving the diagnosis, only this time we cried in celebration.

After listening to the message over and over, I went to the computer to do some research on renal oncocytoma and found even more evidence that I really did experience a miraculous healing. The tumor I had is usually found in men in their late 60's, and the tumors are almost always asymptomatic—without symptoms. My tumor was definitely not asymptomatic—I had all the symptoms of cancer.

The article stated that radiologists could usually distinguish that type of benign tumor from renal cancer because of the presence of a central scar on the tumor. Both of my CAT scans revealed no such scar. As I read further, I got chills. One site's information stated these tumors were so rare in the adrenal gland that there were only 30 reported cases in the literature. After reading that, I knew my chance of having that type of tumor in both the adrenal gland and the kidney was similar to winning the lottery—twice!

We waited anxiously at the door for the girls to come home, and when we heard them drive up under the carport. I ran up to them crying as they stepped out of the car.

Katelyn saw me crying, maybe thinking the worst. "What's wrong Mama?"

"It's not cancer!"

Katelyn shouted, "How do you know? Did the doctor call?"

"Yes, baby, he called and gave us the news this afternoon."

Brittany grabbed and hugged me. I saw the burden of her own private pain during the long weeks of wait fall off of her.

I called everyone I could think of who had been praying for me to let them know that God had said, "Yes," to our prayers.

That night I went into the bathroom to get ready for bed and smiled at the paper taped to the mirror. The words had given me such hope. I read them again out loud.

"He is Able! He wants us to ask for specific things. Sometimes He says, "no," "yes," and "wait."

I went to the kitchen and got a marker out of the drawer and brought it back to the bathroom. I crossed out the words "no" and "wait." All that remained were the words, "God is able. Sometimes He answers yes." Then I added the words, "and He did."

During my quiet time before I went to bed, I read in the book of Joshua where the Lord asked him to take twelve stones and pile them up as a monument to remember the miracle God had performed for His people in bringing them into their Promised Land. I closed my Bible, went into the bathroom, and took down the sheet of paper. I cut out the words that reminded me of God's power. Then I took a piece of red construction paper and cut out a rectangle the size of a bookmark. I glued the words onto the red paper. This would be my marker, my monument, to remind me daily of the miracle He performed in my life. I placed it in my Bible in the book of Mark next to the story of the woman who touched Jesus' garment and was healed.

I HAD SEEN God answer my prayers with "yes" during my life, but I had also seen my prayers answered with "no." He helped me make it through those times when it wasn't in His will to perform a miracle, yet I can honestly say I sensed His presence during the "no times" just as strongly as I sensed it during the times of my miracles.

When Daddy was diagnosed with cancer, many prayers were offered up to the Lord on behalf of him just like the prayers that were offered up at my prayer service. We certainly prayed for a miracle, but it was not God's will to heal him—not because we lacked faith. It's just that God is not a genie. He does not always do things the way we desire Him to do them. I had faith that He would heal me, and He did. I cannot explain why He chose to answer my prayers of healing with "yes," and my daddy's prayers of healing with, "no," but I know that His plan is always perfect even when I don't understand it.

Reading my Bible and praying in bed one night, I became so overcome with thankfulness for what my Savior had done for me that I wrote a poem about His goodness:

> *I praise the Lord for all He's done,*
> *I thank Him daily for sending His Son.*

He held me up those many times I was down,
He saved my soul, I was lost but now I'm found.

Thank you Lord for healing me.
Thank you for drawing me close to Thee.
The valleys are sometimes long and often deep,
It's through my tears Your will I seek.

Blessed be Your holy name!
Life through Christ I now claim.
Help me daily to live for You.

Cleanse me, mold me, and make my heart new!

I knew that I'd be traveling into many more valleys on the road of life, but I'd also stand on more mountaintops as well. My prayer each night after my surgery was that no matter where I happened to be traveling, I would never lose the closeness with my Savior again. The bookmark still helps me do that by reminding me of how much I need the Savior each and every day through all the circumstances of life.

One night after returning from a post-op visit in Houston, the girls came into the bedroom to tell us goodnight as if they, too, had risen above their own valley.

"Mama, Katelyn and I have decided we want to plan our first pool party."

"Oh, is that right?"

"We think we should let Daddy grill hamburgers, and then we can invite everybody over to swim."

Todd put his laptop down and said, "You do know it's a little early to plan a pool party, right? We have about six more months before we can even think about getting in the pool. I think it's late, and we can plan a pool party in a few months."

I smiled as I looked over at him and said, "Let them stay. I think it's the perfect time to plan a party!"

Chapter 13

STORIES OF FAITH

$\mathscr{W}$E ALL NEED cheerleaders, and my friends at work tried to be just that. When I returned to work they greeted me with smiles, hugs, and well wishes for a bright future. In the midst of all the conversation, one of my coworkers said, "Debbie, we were so thankful when we heard your good news. I know you had to be so relieved."

"I was definitely relieved and so thankful to the Lord."

"I hate that you had to think that you had cancer when you really didn't, though. Just think, you worried all that time for no reason."

She didn't realize it, but her words cut right through my spirit. For the first time I realized some people believed there had never been any cancer in my body.

They were thrilled about my good report, but they thought I had won a kind of jackpot of good luck, which took away the miracle that really happened. She was so happy for me, but my heart still shattered into little pieces. I looked into her eyes and said, "Oh, but I did have cancer. There is no doubt in my mind that God healed me from cancer."

She smiled, and even though she and others probably still don't believe me, I know that I touched the hem of Jesus' garment and that He healed me for a reason. He provided answers and opened doors for my family during the search for my sister's killer, and now I experienced His miraculous healing power as He cured me from the disease of cancer.

Yes, God is still in the business of performing miracles today, just as He did 2,000 years ago through His own Son and through the great men of God throughout the ages.

WHILE I WAS on the mountain, others I loved were beginning their journey into the valley. Just a few short months after God healed me, Brother Cal's daughter was diagnosed with leukemia and even on the brink of death when they arrived at St. Jude's hospital. Brother Cal told me that the faith and the miracle he had witnessed in my life helped strengthen his family's faith for the trials they would still have to face with their little girl.

In God's word, he tells us, "What a wonderful God we have—He is the Father of our Lord Jesus Christ, the source of every mercy, and the one who so wonderfully comforts and strengthens us in our hardships and trials. And why does he do this? So that when others are troubled, needing our sympathy and encouragement, we can pass on to them this same help and comfort God has given us."[9]

When we look to the faith that others had before us, it helps strengthen our own faith. This was true in the crowd of people with the woman who touched Jesus' hem. A man named Jairus asked Jesus to heal his twelve year-old daughter who was at the point of death. Jesus was walking with Jairus to his home when the woman in the crowd touched Him. Through her miracle, perhaps Jairus' faith was strengthened to believe in the divine healing of his own daughter, which he needed more than ever. While healing the woman with the issue of blood, the daughter of Jairus died and the people had lost hope, but Jesus said, "Do not fear, only believe." Through Jairus' faith working within the will of God, Jesus raised his daughter back to life. Perhaps the fact that Brother Cal and his family witnessed my miracle just months before they would need their own miracle helped give them the type of faith that Jairus possessed.

Likewise, the great men of faith that I read about growing up—Abraham, Moses, Peter, Paul—helped to strengthen my faith as I went through my struggle with cancer. I have always been in awe of Abraham's life. He would become the father of God's chosen people, but first he had to prove his faith. God asked Abraham to take his son, Isaac, whom He miraculously provided to him and his wife at their old age and do the unthinkable—offer him as a sacrifice. Abraham could have said no, but he trusted God with the life of his son and made the journey to where the sacrifice would take place. As Abraham prepared to kill his son, the Angel of God stopped him and provided a ram standing in a nearby thicket bush to sacrifice instead of his child.

Abraham had such strong faith in the perfect plan of God that he was willing to give everything back to God, including his son. While he was obedient in following God's will, I'm sure in his heart he was hoping for another way. That is exactly how I felt.

Even if cancer claimed my life, I would still have faith in God's perfect will, but I was definitely praying for a different outcome.

Throughout my entire battle with cancer, I prayed to have faith like Abraham, but so often I didn't. Thankfully, Jesus did not require me to have Abrahamic faith. He said, "I tell you the truth, if you had faith even as small as a mustard seed, you could say to this mountain, 'Move from here to there,' and it would move. Nothing would be impossible."[10] My faith probably resembled the mustard seed more than a blossoming tree, but it was enough to lead me to believe that God could remove the cancer if He chose to do so, and He did.

I could say that now, but why did He choose to do it and would I have faith to travel through the valley again if I had to? I would soon find out.

Chapter 14

A NUDGE FROM GOD

Four years after my healing, my left foot swelled just like it had done before. Even after I propped it up at the end of the day, the swelling returned.

"This can't be happening again. God, please let the swelling go away."

For several days I would look down at my foot praying that it would be normal, but each time I checked, I saw swelling. Even though I didn't feel that impending doom that consumed my every thought like I had felt before, I still couldn't help but wonder if I was about to strike out on another journey of faith. I knew all things were possible with God because I had experienced firsthand His mercy and grace through the miracle He provided for me. My faith had been tested and had been strengthened through it all.

This time, I didn't delay in making an appointment with Dr. Cox.

"Well, Mrs. Wilson, what can I do for you today?"

"I wanted you to take a look at my foot, Dr. Cox. It has started swelling again, just like it did when I had the tumor in my right kidney."

He took a look at my foot. "Well, I'm not sure what's going on, but I think we should do a CAT scan to take a look at your left kidney to make sure there are no problems with it."

I followed the same procedure as before and took the film back for him to look at it, but this time as I held the CD in my hand on the short drive to his office, I didn't feel like it foretold my death sentence. I had no scary premonitions, either, but I was still concerned about the outcome of the tests.

Upon my return, I sat in his office quietly fidgeting in the hard plastic chair. I couldn't help but think about how I had been sitting in the exact same chair feeling a similar anxiety almost four years earlier.

This time, Mother sat next to me instead of Todd. My thoughts jumped to how determined he sounded on the phone to get back to town from his job in Florida.

"Are you having any symptoms other than the swelling?"

"No, I don't have any pain in my side or anything."

"You're not keeping anything from me are you?"

"No, I promise that is the only symptom I'm experiencing."

"Well, it's going to take me about ten hours to make it home, but I'm on my way now."

"Todd, you really don't have to come home. I'll be fine. I've made the appointment with Dr. Cox, and I promise I'll call you as soon as I get out of his office. Besides, Mother promised she would go with me to the appointment."

"I'm coming home, Debbie, and you can't say anything that will make me change my mind."

I prayed that he would take his time so that he would soon be safely by my side even though he wouldn't get home in time to hear the test results with me. We were miles apart, but I knew he was praying for me as I waited to hear what Dr. Cox had to say.

Mother was anxious, too. She wondered if Dr. Cox would deliver the same diagnosis of cancer as he had done before. After all, I had the same symptom—the foot swelling that caused Todd to make me promise to make an appointment with Dr. Cox. Everything seemed like a replay of my first diagnosis.

Once again, I felt as though the brown paneled

walls were closing in on me. I stood up and walked over to the wall to look at the family portraits and the framed Bible verse from Isaiah that I had read before.

> Have you not known? Have you not heard? The everlasting God, the Lord, The Creator of the ends of the earth, neither faints nor is weary, His understanding is unsearchable. He gives power to the weak, and to those who have no might He increases strength. Even the youths shall faint and be weary, And the young men shall utterly fall, But those that wait upon the Lord shall renew their strength; They shall mount up with wings as eagles; They shall run, and not be weary; and They shall walk, and not faint.[11]

After reading the passage, tears filled my eyes because I knew my hope was in the Lord, and I knew that no matter what the CAT scan results were, God would be with me just as He had been with me four years earlier when He had given me my miracle. He would give me strength in my time of weakness. My feelings of fear left me, and I was overcome by a hope that only the Savior can give.

I wondered if God put me in that chair again to help me clearly remember the fears and anxiety that transformed into peace and hope-filled faith, so I could tell others about my hope in God. I felt as if He wanted me to do that for four years, but I had been ignoring His will, continuing on my own path—maybe even becoming complacent again. Perhaps He wanted me in a dark place for a few days, just as He put Jonah in the dark belly of the fish, to get my attention and start obeying.

I promised the Lord right then, *"If you allow me to once again be free of cancer, I will write my story—my miracle—your miracle, so all will read about your goodness and faithfulness and . . . "* The door swung open. Dr. Cox walked in and sat across from us at his desk still stacked high with medical books and papers.

"Mrs. Wilson, I looked at your report, and your kidney is fine. I think your symptoms are related to some scar tissue from your previous surgery when your kidney was removed."

He wrote on his prescription pad and said, "This prescription should help the swelling."

Mother smiled, and I looked at her with relief.

"I don't see anything remarkable with the kidney. I think it's functioning just fine."

"Thank you, Dr. Cox," I said as I held back the tears of joy.

I hurried outside the office and called Todd. He had been on the road for several hours: "Hey, everything is fine. It's just some scar tissue that's causing the swelling. I hope you don't think I'm crazy for saying this, but I think I know why this happened."

"What do you mean?"

"Everything happened just like before. God put me back with the same symptom, same chair, same tests so I could remember those raw emotions, the anxiety, the need to be dependent on Him so I could write about it."

Todd didn't say anything for a few minutes. The same emotions had come racing back to him, too, and he couldn't speak.

"How much longer before you get here?"

"I should be there before you get home from church tonight."

During the ride home after the mid-week church service, I thought about how close I grew to God while in the cancer valley and how I had relied on Him to help me get through every minute of each day, even when the voice inside told me to give up. I vowed to never drift from that closeness, but perhaps I had. Perhaps that's another reason God put me in this same position. I wanted that type of relationship even without the diagnosis of cancer. I prayed and asked God to help me always feel that closeness. I renewed my vow to study His word and prayed to keep that bond strong. I wanted to follow His will in everything that I did in my life. I knew I would make mistakes along the way, but I had a new sense of urgency to study and learn more about Him.

When I reached the house, Todd met me under the carport. He smiled, reached out to me, and held me for several minutes. Then he told me how much he loved me.

"I'm sorry I got you all upset for nothing."

"Well, at least I got to come home from work early."

We both laughed and went in the house. The next morning I walked into the bathroom and made my daily trip to the scale in my closet to check for any unwanted new pounds. I stepped up and looked down at the digital display. I stared with wide eyes and open mouth—not at the number of pounds, but at my feet.

"Come look at this," I laughed, calling out to Todd.

"What's funny?"

"It's not really funny, but just look."

"What am I looking at? Have you lost a bunch of weight or gained some?"

"No, look at my feet."

"What about them?"

"They are the same size! There is no more swelling."

"They do look the same size."

"And I haven't even taken any medication for it, because we didn't get the prescription filled yet. You know, I really believe God wants me to write about my miracle, and I've been so stubborn, because I just didn't want to do it. He keeps putting signs all around me, and I just haven't been listening to Him."

When Todd left the room, I sat down on my vanity chair where I put on my makeup and just stared into the mirror. I glanced over to the spot where I had kept that piece of paper for so many months. The words that I used to read each morning and evening flashed before me: "He is Able! He wants us to ask for specific things. Sometimes He says, "no," "yes," and "wait."

"God, I will no longer say "no" to your will. I won't even ask for you to "wait." I will say, "yes" and obey you."

I finished getting dressed and headed to work, but my mood was very different than it had been for quite some time. I sang all the way to the office. My song erupted from the joy that I again had in my heart—not because the doctor told me I didn't have cancer, even though that was wonderful news. I had the joy of knowing that I would be in the center of God's will, not my own.

Even though following His will meant long hours of working on manuscripts, spending money for the necessary editing and promoting of a new book, and many other things that I didn't particularly enjoy doing, I had the kind of peace in my heart that the apostle Paul described:

> Always be full of joy in the Lord; I say it again, rejoice! Let everyone see that you are unselfish and considerate in all you do. Remember that the Lord is coming soon. Don't worry about anything; instead, pray about everything; tell God your needs and don't forget to thank him for his answers. If you do this you will experience God's peace, which is far more wonderful than the human mind can understand. His peace will keep your thoughts and your hearts quiet and at rest as you trust in Christ Jesus.[12]

When I pulled into my parking spot at work and turned off the car, I prayed: *"God, I praise you for all that you have done for me. Your blessings on my family are never-ending. I want to be in the center of your will. I know that is the only place that I will ever have true peace and joy. If it truly is your will for me to write about the miracle you performed in my life, please Lord, let me know beyond a shadow of a doubt. Give me just one more sign that will confirm what you would have me to do."*

Around noon that day, Todd called to ask if I wanted to meet him for lunch at Slaydens, one of our favorite local restaurants. Just as we were finishing our meal, a lady walked up to our table and smiled at me. She looked familiar, but I couldn't remember her name.

"Remember me? I'm Susan Brent from the book club. Remember, you came and spoke to our group about your book, *Sweet Scent of Justice*."

"Oh, yes, I remember. I really enjoyed talking to your group. How have you been?"

"I've been doing great."

"What book is the group reading now?"

"We just started reading a book another local author has written." She went on to tell me a little bit about it.

"We sure enjoyed reading your book. It touched the hearts of so many of the women in our group. It was wonderful hearing you speak that night. Do you think you will ever write another book? You really should. We would definitely put it on our book list if you did."

"Well, as a matter of fact, I've been thinking and praying about doing just that."

We talked for a few more minutes while my face

beamed with joy. I knew I had my sign from God. When she walked away, I thought, *"Lord, you didn't waste any time answering that prayer!"*

It was time to face my fears just like Jonah had done after being delivered from the great fish. He had a mission to deliver a specific message to the people of Nineveh—I now have a mission to deliver a message to as many people as I can reach—that God still performs miracles, and even more importantly, when we depend on Him through our trials, He is always faithful and good to us. I had no more doubt. It was time to embark upon my mission.

The prophet Isaiah once said, "How beautiful on the mountains are the feet of the messenger who brings good news, the good news of peace and salvation, the news that the God of Israel reigns!"[13] I am so honored to stand on the mountain as God's publisher of His good news of peace and salvation for your soul to hear.

ACKNOWLEDGMENTS

*G*OD HAS BLESSED my life with so many wonderful people who supported me and stood by my side through my entire ordeal. Each of them gave me courage and strength as I walked through that dark valley.

To my church family and Brother Cal, thank you for the visits, the calls, and the cards during my illness. Most of all, thank you for going before the Lord with prayers for my healing. Your prayers along with the prayers of others were heard and answered by the Savior.

To my family who never wavered in showing me unconditional love and encouragement. You prayed so faithfully, and you never showed fear even though I knew you were worried and concerned.

To Brittany and Katelyn, thank you for loving me. It was so difficult to think that I might miss out on so many important events in your lives, but I knew that because you both had a relationship with the Lord, you would be able to continue on without me even if God had not performed a miracle in my life. I am thankful for your faith in God.

To Todd, you are my rock. God made you just for me, and my life would be incomplete without you. I love you with all my heart, and I pray that God will continue to give us many more years together.

Thank you, Lord, for saving me. You could have chosen to take me from this earth, but by faith I believe you healed me of my cancer. I give you all the glory and honor for my miracle.

VERSES CONCERNING FAITH

I've always heard that in our Christian walk we are either entering a valley, in a valley, or coming out of a valley. During each of these phases of life we can be certain that through our faith in God, He can give us the strength, courage, and hope that we need to travel along the road of life.

The following verses found in God's word remind us that faith is the key to not only this life, but also eternal life that is found in Jesus Christ. Meditating on them helps to strengthen my daily walk with Him. My hope is that you will also find them a source of encouragement in your walk as well.

"You can never please God without faith, without depending on him. Anyone who wants to come to God must believe that there is a God and that he rewards those who sincerely look for him."

(Hebrews 11:6)

"So Jesus answered and said to them, "Assuredly, I say to you, if you have faith and do not doubt, you will not only do what was done to the fig tree, but also if you say to this mountain, 'Be removed and be cast into the sea,' it will be done."

(Matthew 21:21)

"And those whose faith has made them good in God's sight must live by faith, trusting him in everything. Otherwise, if they shrink back, God will have no pleasure in them."

(Hebrews 10:38)

"What is faith? It is the confident assurance that something we want is going to happen. It is the certainty that what we hope for is waiting for us, even though we cannot see it up ahead."

(Hebrews 11:1-2)

"If your faith were only the size of a mustard seed," Jesus answered, "it would be large enough to uproot that mulberry tree over there and send

Verses Concerning Faith

it hurtling into the sea! Your command would bring immediate results!"

(Luke 17:6)

"I can do all things through Christ who strengthens me."

(Philippians 4:13 KJV)

"These trials are only to test your faith, to see whether or not it is strong and pure. It is being tested as fire tests gold and purifies it—and your faith is far more precious to God than mere gold; so if your faith remains strong after being tried in the test tube of fiery trials, it will bring you much praise and glory and honor on the day of his return."

(1 Peter 1:7)

"If you want to know what God wants you to do, ask him, and he will gladly tell you, for he is always ready to give a bountiful supply of wisdom to all who ask him; he will not resent it. But when you ask him, be sure that you really expect him to tell you, for a doubtful mind will be as unsettled as a wave of the sea that is driven and tossed by the wind; and every decision you then make will be uncertain, as you turn first this way, and then that. **If you don't ask with**

faith, don't expect the Lord to give you any solid answer."
(JAMES 1:5-8, EMPHASIS MINE)

"For we live by believing and not by seeing."
(2 CORINTHIANS 5:7)

"For you know that when your faith is tested, your endurance has a chance to grow. So let it grow, for when your endurance is fully developed, you will be perfect and complete, needing nothing."
(JAMES 1:3–4)

"So faith comes from hearing, that is, hearing the Good News about Christ."
(ROMANS 10:17)

"For every child of God defeats this evil world, and we achieve this victory through our faith."
(1 JOHN 5:4)

"God saved you by his grace when you believed. And you can't take credit for this; it is a gift from God."
(EPHESIANS 2:8)

"Therefore, put on every piece of God's armor so you will be able to resist the enemy in the time of evil. Then after the battle you will still be standing firm. Stand your ground, putting on the belt of truth and the body armor of God's righteousness. For shoes, put on the peace that comes from the Good News so that you will be fully prepared. In addition to all of these, hold up the shield of **faith** to stop the fiery arrows of the devil."

(EPHESIANS 6:13–16)

"Through Christ you have come to trust in God. And you have placed your faith and hope in God because he raised Christ from the dead and gave him great glory."

(1 PETER 1:21)

"Be on guard. Stand firm in the faith. Be courageous. Be strong."

(1 CORINTHIANS 16:13)

"But we who live by the Spirit eagerly wait to receive by faith the righteousness God has promised to us."

(GALATIANS 5:5)

"Therefore, since we are surrounded by such a huge crowd of witnesses to the life of faith, let us strip off every weight that slows us down, especially the sin that so easily trips us up. And let us run with endurance the race God has set before us. We do this by keeping our eyes on Jesus, the champion who initiates and perfects our faith. Because of the joy awaiting him, he endured the cross, disregarding its shame. Now he is seated in the place of honor beside God's throne."

(HEBREWS 12:1-2)

(A picture of our family in New York City after appearing on the show, "On the Case with Paula Zahn" for my book, *Sweet Scent of Justice.)*

ANSWERS FROM THE AUTHOR

Why does God allow bad things to happen to good people?

I don't think we will ever know for sure why certain things happen in our lives until we get to heaven. There are times when our own sin causes us to suffer. Then there are times when there is no real answer as to why we must experience pain and suffering. I do know that in God's word He tells us that some events take place in order for God to be glorified. That was the case with many of the healings that took place in the Bible. God received the glory after all hope had been lost. Through telling my own true stories, I believe that God is receiving glory for the miracles He performed in my life.

Was the voice of death and destruction in the beginning of your journey from God?

If the voice came from God, it would have come with a peaceful assurance, not such condemnation. Also, in His word, it says that the enemy of God (the devil) is the father of lies. It is his number one goal to destroy the children of God from having assurance that they will go to heaven. His second goal is to keep God's children from telling others about His great goodness and love. I was already a believer and assured of eternity, so the enemy wanted to keep me from telling you about our Father in heaven and how you and I can meet there one day. Without faith, prayer, and reliance on God, I would have had faith in the voice, instead, and the enemy of my soul may have succeeded in his plan to take me out of this earth, and this book would not be in your hands.

How can I have assurance that I will one day go to heaven?

John 14:6 says, "I am the way, the truth, and the life. No one can come to the Father except through me."

Jesus is the only way to heaven. God loved us so much that He sent His only son to die upon a cross so that we could be saved. Christ took on the sins of the world when He was crucified, and because of His unconditional love we can all receive the free gift of salvation. If you are willing to admit that you are a sinner, repent of your sins, and believe that He died to save you, you can receive the gift of salvation. Sincerely tell the Lord these things. Ask Him to enter your life and take over your heart. Have faith that He will save you, and you will experience His love and forgiveness. He will come into your life and dwell within you, and your life will begin anew.

You can contact me at debbiewilson.org for additional information about my experience and for answers to other questions you might have.

$\mathcal{D}$EBBIE WILSON, THE author of *Sweet Scent of Justice* and *Even in the Valley,* has been an educator for over twenty-eight years. She is currently serving as a New Teacher Induction Coordinator where she provides professional development to new teachers entering the teaching profession. She also teaches online classes at a local college where she received her undergraduate degree in Elementary Education, her Master's Degree in Elementary Education, and her certification in the area of Administration and Supervision. She has been married to Todd, her high school sweetheart, for over twenty-eight years, and they have two beautiful daughters, Brittany and Katelyn. Debbie can be contacted at debbiewilson.org.

ENDNOTES

1. Psalm 23:4, KJV
2. Matthew 14:22–33, NLT
3. Matthew 18:20
4. "Shout to the Lord," written by Darlene Zschech,© 1993 Hillsong Publishing / Thankyou Music; © 1993, DarleneZschech/Hillsong Publishing, admin. Integrity's Hosanna! Music
5. *"Even in the Valley,"written by Rebecca J. Peck & Amy Marie Unthank (http://www.rebeccapeck.net)*
   (c) Copyright Thomas Peck Music (BMI). Reprinted with permission.
6. John 3:16, KJV
7. Hebrews 11:32-38
8. Job 41:8–11
9. 2 Corinthians 1:3–4
10. Matthew 17:20, KJV
11. Isaiah 40:28–31, unknown translation.
12. Philippians 4:4–8
13. Isaiah 52:7

www.ingramcontent.com/pod-product-compliance
Lightning Source LLC
LaVergne TN
LVHW040115080426
835507LV00039B/374